Frontier Teachers

Frontier Teachers

Stories of Heroic Women
of the Old West

Chris Enss

Guilford, Connecticut

Helena, Montana

To buy books in quantity for corporate use
or incentives, call **(800) 962–0973**
or e-mail **premiums@GlobePequot.com**.

A · T W O D O T® · B O O K

TwoDot is a registered trademark of Morris Book Publishing, LLC.

Text design by Libby Kingsbury

Library of Congress Cataloging-in-Publication Data is available on file.

ISBN 978-0-7627-4819-8

Printed in the United States of America

10 9 8 7 6 5 4 3 2

*For Sarah B. Stamm and Virginia Upton, teachers who
spurred me on and inspired my love for the written word;
and for Deb Frank, a gracious teacher who makes
a difference every day.*

Contents

Foreword

Throughout history teachers have been at the forefront of all civilizations, educating and inspiring the next generation and keeping societies moving forward. *Frontier Teachers* artfully captures that pioneering, resilient, and enduring spirit of teachers that lives on today.

These women, many at the ripe old age of sixteen or eighteen, were trailblazers. They risked it all—traveling thousands of miles on crude trails through wilderness, across deserts, and over mountain passes—not just for the promise of a better future for themselves, but for the opportunity to bring education and the joy of learning to the children of the western frontier. They did as much to settle the Wild West as celebrated lawmen, gold seekers, and the railroad.

The women of the West broke the male stranglehold on the teaching profession, which was dominated by men on the East Coast. Today, more than 70 percent of teachers are women. And although, sadly, it took one hundred years, the descendants of these pioneers, through union organizing, established the single-salary schedule that finally guaranteed female teachers equal pay for equal work, passed a collective-bargaining law to give teachers a voice in their profession, and boldly made it so female teachers couldn't be fired for simply getting married.

In many ways we've come a long way since the 1800s, but strong similarities to the twenty-first century remain. These women were more than scholars. They were town leaders who first had to find a location for the schoolhouse and then raise the money to build it. They scrambled to find adequate textbooks—often using their own salaries to buy additional materials or provide books to students who couldn't afford them. And they struggled to ensure that all children, including those who didn't speak English as their native language, had the opportunity to learn and improve their lives.

I'm proud to be a second-generation teacher. My mother and father taught me that public education is the soul of our society and the key to our future. In telling the hardships and triumphs of these early educators, Chris Enss reminds all of us that we owe it to ourselves and our children to celebrate the joy of teaching and learning every day.

—David A. Sanchez
President, California Teachers Association

Acknowledgments

Many librarians and historians assisted me in compiling the information for this book. The completion of this material would not have been possible without the assistance of Joyce M. Cox, head of reference services at the Nevada State Library and Archives, and the staff at the California State Library. I'm grateful to Ellie Arguimbau at the Montana Historical Society, Ed Tyson at Searls Library in Nevada City, California, and all the courthouses and city halls in New Mexico, San Antonio, Texas, and Denver, Colorado.

Many people have been of immense help and inspiration during the writing of this book. They include, but are certainly not limited to, Cissy Murphy and Patti Ferree, my friends and encouragers; Mary Ann Trygg at the Nevada County Public Library and her generous staff and the volunteers there; Dakota and Sunny Livesay at Chronicles of the Old West for their support and kindness; and Erin Turner for the opportunities she has extended to me as an author for Globe Pequot Press.

Introduction

"In their way pioneer women were the molders and shapers of western society;
mothers, wives, business owners, schoolmarms, slowly but surely exerting their
influence on the cities, towns, and communities in which they lived."

—Utah pioneer and suffragette,
Emmeline B. Wells, 1897

A warm noonday sun shone down on a small log schoolhouse near the base of an imposing mountain overlooking the Missoula Valley in Montana in 1878. A faint, blue sky stretched endlessly over the structure and a belt of lush green timber surrounded it. The windows of the building were open and a breeze filtered gently into the single room that contained eleven eager students. Olive Pickering, a young, demure teacher from New Hampshire, sat behind her desk reading aloud to her class. Her students were enthralled with the story and hung on every word.

A slight movement from something outside the glass window suddenly caught Olive's eyes, and she looked up from the McGuffey Reader toward a fence that encircled the school. Several Native Americans from the Salish tribe were perched on the post, listening intently to the lesson.

Olive smiled at their attentiveness and continued on with the recitation.

The story that fascinated both her pupils and the Indians involved three boys who attended a boarding school. The mother of each boy sent him a nice cake. The first boy hid his cake in his bedroom and ate until it was gone. He became very ill and had to go to the doctor. The second boy put his cake away, nibbled on it occasionally and joyfully anticipated nibbling still more, but in the meantime the mice found it and made short work of it. The third boy called in his friends and gave each a generous slice, thereby setting a good example for his classmates.

Olive concluded the lesson and dismissed the class. She watched the Indians linger by the window for a bit, and then they headed off to their homes. She waved goodbye to her students and the Salish, pleased they had been so interested and confident they had learned something.

Beginning in 1846, hordes of settlers and their families traveled by land and water and converged on the West from all points of the compass. In their ardent hunt for gold to mine and fertile land to farm and ranch, they explored or settled every nook of the region from Nome, Alaska, to Santa Fe, New Mexico.

Towns sprang into existence with the influx of people; churches were formed, laws were enacted, and schools were established. Concerned parents realized that they needed to establish a formal education system. "Schools are necessary and good teachers along with them," Mary Havens, a settler to Carson Valley, California, stated in 1863. "Without them our children will become orphans of progress."

Pioneers who felt the same had the foresight to set aside land where schools could be built and later sought contributions from residents for the upkeep on the schoolhouses and supplies for the pupils.

Among the population pushing beyond the boundaries of the Mississippi River were daring female educators who hoped to find work teaching frontier boys and girls how to read and write. All that was initially required of teachers was that they be able to count, read,

Courtesy of Library of Congress, LC=US262=2132

Frontier schoolmistress Blanch LaMont poses with her students at the one-room schoolhouse in Hecla, Montana, in 1893.

write, and mend a pen. But these new schoolmarms were energetic, and they arrived able to do immeasurably more than the basics.

Although some emigrants felt it was only proper that a school-master teach their children how to read and write, the scarcity of professionals of either gender on the frontier made it impractical to turn away women who offered essential services. According to an 1890 census, 11 percent of the country's female teachers lived in the West. Although studies conducted by the National Popular Education Board in the 1870s showed that pupils under women teachers had improved more than those taught by men, schoolmarms were still paid less. Women educators were paid an average of $54.50 a year. Schoolmasters were paid $71.40.

Educational pioneers like Catherine Beecher and Mary Lyons encouraged ladies to enter the field and take their talent into uncharted territory. Beecher spoke out against the traditional role of women in the nineteenth century and the popular notion that men made better teachers because they could be more firm with students resistant to studying.

Between 1847 and 1858, more than six hundred female teachers traveled across the untamed frontier to provide youngsters with an education. There were few opportunities for respectable work for women in the early 1800s. For those women who did not want the socially acceptable career as a seamstress or nurse, there was teaching. It was the most popular profession for women in the 1840s.

For Luella Fergus, a fourteen-year-old girl living in Illinois, it was the only thing she wanted to do. The prospective educator's father was living in the Montana territory in 1862 when she wrote him a letter about the requirements needed to enter the field.

"Teaching school is all the talk among young ladies," Luella wrote, "if they can do sums and fractions they can teach."

Women like Sister Blandina Segale taught in the New Mexico territory in the 1880s for virtually no pay. Any funds that were donated to her for her work she turned back into the school to be used to purchase writing utensils, books, and upgrades to the schoolhouse. Sarah Royce initially agreed to teach children the three Rs in her home in Grass Valley, California, in 1857 in exchange for homemade preserves and chicken eggs. The motivation for these women to endure such want and hardship was to improve the minds of boys and girls in a new land.

Even the teachers who did receive a regular salary felt that educating youngsters was necessary for the betterment of mankind. Some believed it was divine duty. Michigan-born Flora Davis Winslow, who left home to teach school in the Colorado territory in 1875, echoed that sentiment in her journal: "I teach school because I wish to be independent and not beholding to my friends for a livelihood. I go west to do the will of my Heavenly Father."

The women included in this volume demonstrated the level of dedication and sacrifice needed to bring formal education to the settlements beyond the Mississippi River. For many students their teachers were heroic figures who introduced them to a world of possibilities.

The educators contained in this book were resourceful, tenacious, and fearless. Olive Mann Isbell and Hannah Clapp came to class armed with guns in order to keep their students safe from hostile Indians who threatened to harm them.

Mary McLench Gray and Lucia Darling trekked hundreds of miles over treacherous country to bring their gift of teaching to boys and girls in the most remote areas of the western region. Limited schoolbooks and supplies did not stop teachers like Eliza Mott from helping children to learn to read. She taught the alphabet to her students using the inscriptions on tombstones at a nearby cemetery.

Pioneer communities grew in prosperity and stability as a result of the work of early teachers. "It was the pursuit of knowledge under difficulties," one educator remembered in her journal in 1871, "but we made time count for all that."

Many more educators displayed courage in ways other than their fearless undertaking of rough westward journeys. In addition to her talent for teaching, Elizabeth Thorn Scott possessed a daring drive to see to it that neglected children in black communities had an opportunity to learn as well as the children of white settlers. In 1854, she opened the first African-American school in Sacramento. Elizabeth, a widow with three children who had moved to California from New Bedford, Massachusetts, taught fourteen pupils in a small classroom in the basement of her home. By 1859 the number of pupils enrolled at the school was more than two hundred.

Swedish born teacher Elise Amalie Waerenskjold immigrated to the Texas panhandle in 1847, without a teaching position, and helped raise money to build the first school in the small town of Hamilton. She later wrote about her experiences as a teacher. The volume, entitled *The Lady with the Pen*, was used as a training manual for other educators.

Ambitious Elizabeth Millar Wilson traveled to the Oregon territory in 1851 in hopes of educating the native Chinook people. After learning to speak the language, she took a teaching position at the reservation and later made public accounts of her encounters with the Indians and her experiences teaching in the West.

Without the schoolmarms who came over the plains to be instruments of good, westward advancement would have stagnated. "Without women's moral influence as teachers on the frontier," Sarah Josepha Hale, the editor of *Godey's Lady's Book* wrote in 1870, "gold would have proved to be a curse and not a blessing."

The school bell has been rung, the doors closed, and the readers distributed. The pages that follow reveal the accomplishments of twelve fearless teachers and celebrate the value they placed on learning. Class is now in session.

Sister Blandina Segale

THE OUTLAW'S TEACHER

"Today my capacity for controlling them was put to the test. You know I'm a companion outside of the schoolroom, and a teacher the instant the threshold of the schoolroom is crossed."

—SISTER BLANDINA SEGALE'S COMMENTS ABOUT
THE OLDER AND MUCH TALLER PUPILS
IN HER CLASS, JANUARY 10, 1873

Sister Blandina stood over the pale, bullet-ridden body of a young gunman and mopped the sweat off his brow with a white cloth. He smiled benignly up at her, then turned his attention to the outlaws surrounding his bed. The renegades stared back at him quietly, all wearing grave expressions that reflected the severity of his physical condition. Sister Blandina's eyes shifted from the injured youth to the teenage boy standing next to him, tapping his holstered gun with his hat. "Sister Blandina," the weak patient began, "Billy, our captain . . . ."

Teenage outlaw Billy the Kid nodded politely to the nun. "We are glad to see you, sister, and I want to say, it would give me pleasure to be able to do you any favor."

For more than a month Sister Blandina had been caring for the wounded member of Billy the Kid's gang known only as Happy Jack. After being shot in the thigh he had been dumped in an

1

Sister Blandina Segale

abandoned adobe hut near Trinidad, Colorado, and left for dead. A boy from the school where Sister Blandina taught had found him and brought her to the location to help. In addition to fresh bandages and water, she had furnished the hurt desperado with food and linens. She had tended to his spiritual as well as physical needs, and for that she was rewarded with an audience with Happy Jack's partner in crime.

"He has steel-blue eyes and a peach complexion," she recalled later in her journal. ". . . One would take him to be seventeen—innocent looking, save for the corners of his eyes, which tell a set purpose, good or bad."

The purpose Sister Blandina had learned for one of Billy's upcoming rides was definitely bad. According to Jack, the gang was going to kill the four physicians living in the area who had refused to call on the gunshot gang member. She was thinking of those men when she exchanged cordialities with Billy.

"Yes, there is a favor you can grant me," she said responding to his offer.

"He reached his hand toward me," she recounted later. "The favor is granted," the Kid promised.

She went on to recall, "I took the hand saying, 'I understand you have come to scalp our Trinidad physicians, which act I ask you to cancel.' After a quick moment contemplating the request, Billy said. 'I granted the favor before I knew what it was, and it stands. Not only that, sister,' he continued, 'but at any time my pals and I can serve you, you will find us ready.'"

Sister Blandina thanked him and left the room.

"Life is a mystery," she jotted in her journal. "What of the human heart? A compound of goodness and wickedness. Who has ever solved the secret of its workings? I thought: one moment diabolical, the next angelical."

3

When Sister Blandina was first called to Trinidad, she believed the mining town was located in Cuba. It wasn't until she boarded a stage in Cincinnati, Ohio, where she had attended the St. Vincent Academy and taken her holy vows, that she learned she was bound for the territory of Colorado. She had secretly prayed to be sent west to Santa Fe where her order, the Sisters of Charity, had traveled in 1865. Her desire to live and work on the wild frontier was realized in September 1872.

Rosa Maria Segale was born on January 23, 1850, in Cicagna, Italy. She came to America with her parents and three other siblings when she was four years old. The family settled in Cincinnati where several of their other countrymen had made their home. Rosa had a difficult time in Ohio. Not being able to speak the language was a barrier; and apart from her older sisters, she had no one to play with or talk to. It wasn't until her parents arranged for their children to have English lessons that the young girl came into her own.

After finishing school and completing several music and Spanish language courses, Rosa entered a convent. Once she had taken her final vows, she was given the name Sister Blandina. A brief stint teaching in Dayton and Steubenville, Ohio, opened the door to her first westward assignment. Although she was thrilled with the commission, she was sad to be leaving her older sister behind. Maria was two years older than Sister Blandina and was also a nun with the Sisters of Charity order. The two had become very close, and the thought of being apart was devastating. Sister Blandina promised to keep a journal of her experiences for Maria, whose name was changed to Sister Justina, to share with her whenever they were together. Sister Blandina maintained the journal for twenty-one years.

Before Sister Blandina began her long journey alone to Trinidad, she was made aware of the trouble she might encounter along the way and how best to protect herself.

"Sister, you may be snow-bound while on the plains," one of two well-meaning frontiersmen staying over in Ohio explained. "Travelers are sometimes snow-bound for two weeks, and you are alone. This though is not the greatest danger to you. Your real danger is from cowboys . . . no virtuous woman is safe near a cowboy."

"Mentally," Sister Blandina later wrote in her journal, "I was wishing both gentlemen were somewhere else. When I showed no signs of reconsidering the venture, both gave up trying to make me understand what they considered dangerous. Why should snow or cowboys frighten me any more than others who will be traveling the same way!"

The fearless, determined nun arrived at her Colorado destination on December 10, 1872. She was greeted warmly by the other sisters living at the Trinidad convent and learned all about the school where she would be working. She spent the time prior to visiting the facility for herself reviewing her Spanish. She was surprised to find out that the other sisters did not speak the language but encouraged that her example had created a desire for them to want to.

"I am sure, dearest Sister Justina," Sister Blandina's journal entry for December 14, 1872, began, "You will be interested in my viewpoint of things as I find them here."

Today I went to look at my schoolroom to be; 40 feet long; 14 feet wide; 8 feet high; two small windows, low-sized door, solid adobe wall on two sides, log rafters as black as ebony. Any necessary ventilation said "Goodbye" when the house was completed.

School was in session the following month and Sister Blandina's first class consisted of a number of pupils older than the average student she was used to working with. The feisty fifteen- and sixteen-year-old males were mischievous and started out the first day by attempting to play a joke on the new teacher. Speaking only in Spanish they made plans not to return to class after recess. Sister Blandina had overheard the boys and foiled their attempts to leave. The fact that she spoke their language and stood up to them earned her instant respect. She had their full attention for the rest of the day.

"I wonder what the next attempt on the teacher will be," she wrote in her journal, "for boys will be boys all over the world."

The majority of the day-to-day class work centered around addition and subtraction, reading, writing, geography, U.S. history, and the Catholic religion. With the exception of Catholic studies, all of the subjects were required by law to be taught.

Class time was periodically disrupted by attacks from area Ute Indians who were trying to drive out everyone who was not Mexican. The Utes allied themselves with the Mexican people because they did not perceive them as a threat to their way of life.

"They are angry," Sister Blandina conveyed in her daily writing, "because government agents have repeatedly made the tribes 'move on.' Poor Indians! Will they ever understand that the conquerors claim the land? How quickly the Indian detects true sympathy from the counterfeit!"

At the close of the last term, Sister Blandina realized that changes had to be made to the growing school. With the increase in the number of students enrolled came an increase in the number of desks needed. Sister Blandina hired a carpenter to cut the eight-foot-long desks the classroom possessed in half, making two four-foot-long desks in the process. Every child who came to school had a place to sit, but the available space to move around or add more chairs was limited. The sister was compelled to pray that the Lord would "provide the region with a new, much bigger school."

The primitive building had many other uses when school was out. It served as a town meeting place, and the music hall was the favored location for funerals.

Sister Blandina had faith that the residents would consider this fact and contribute to the construction of a new community facility, and that funding would not rest entirely with the local church.

The nuns at the convent were in favor of a new school building but did not have enough cash to pay interest on the debt that would be incurred for such a project.

"They asked me if I had a plan by which I could build without money," Sister Blandina noted in her memoirs dated June 1876. "Here is my plan, I told the Sisters. Borrow a crowbar, get on the roof of the schoolhouse and begin to detach the adobes. The first good Mexican who sees me will ask, 'What are you doing, Sister?' I will answer, 'Tumbling down this structure to rebuild it before the opening of the fall term of school.'"

Sister Blandina wrote in her journal:

You should have seen the sisters laugh! It did me good. After three days pondering how to get rid of low ceilings, poor ventilation, acrobats from log-rafters introduced themselves without notice, and now here is an opportunity to carry out a test on the good in human nature, so I took it. I borrowed a crowbar and went on the roof, detached some adobes and began throwing them down. The school building is only one story high.

The first person who came towards the school house was Dona Juanita Simpson. . . . When she saw me at work she exclaimed, "For the love of God, Sister, what are you doing?" I answered, "We need a school house that will a little resemble those we have in the United States, so I am demolishing this one in order to rebuild." "How many men do you need, Sister?" "We need not only men, but also straw, moulds, hods, shovels—everything to build a house with a shingle

7

roof. Our assets are good-will and energy." Mrs. Simpson returned with six men . . . and in a few days the old building was thrown down, the adobes made and sun-burnt."

In less than a month's time, a stone foundation was laid and a new schoolhouse built on top of it. All the supplies and labor needed to build the facility were donated. The church's bishop arrived for a visit from Denver and was amazed at the generosity of the people in the village and applauded Sister Blandina's efforts to bring the community together for such a purpose.

Sister Blandina's kindness and resourcefulness extended beyond her dedication to teaching. She had a heart for the sick and destitute as well. There was a woeful absence of medical professionals and hospitals in the territory. Sister Blandina had a knack for nursing.

Although she had no formal training in the field, she had witnessed the Sisters of Charity in Ohio nurse wounded soldiers during the Civil War. Her goal was to help build a hospital where Native Americans, orphans, miners, and injured outlaws could receive care. She believed that treating people regardless of their social standing and or available funds was essential for her service to God and the church.

The students at the Trinidad School knew Sister Blandina's position on helping those in need and were unafraid to come to her to ask for assistance. It was one of her pupils who approached her to lend aid to the wounded member of Billy the Kid's gang, Happy Jack.

"He's badly hurt and has a very poor chance of living," the student told her.

"We shall do all we can for him," was the Sister's reply.

Her gracious assistance profoundly changed the heart of the outlaw. She recounted in her journal about the moment Happy Jack surrendered his will:

"Sister, now do you think God can forgive me?" The dying law-breaker asked.

I answered: "Turn to me in sorrow of heart and I will forgive, saith the Lord."

"Sister, I do not doubt that you believe God will forgive me: I'm going to tell you what I think God would do. Through you, God is leading me to ask pardon for my many devilish acts."

Sister Blandina looked after Happy Jack for nine months before he succumbed to his injuries and died.

When the boys and girls in Sister Blandina's class studied long hours to achieve high marks, she rewarded them for their efforts. According to her memoirs, if the children completed their school-work, they were allowed to participate in dramatic and musical presentations. "There are no amusements for the young folks, nor for old ones either, so the school frequently gives entertainments. . . . The fun is enjoyed by all, especially by the parents and friends of the pupils."

In December 1876 Sister Blandina was transferred from the nunnery in Trinidad to a convent in Santa Fe, New Mexico. The citizens of the Colorado town threatened to write the mother superior to ask that the sister be allowed to stay, but the devoted woman would not permit it. She would go where she was called.

"Here's a heart for every fate," she told them.

The stage driver and a reverend assigned to accompany the sister and a fellow nun on her journey were apprehensive about the trip because Billy the Kid's gang was quite active on the plains.

Sister Blandina's previous encounter with Billy led her to believe there was no need for concern. She wrote in her journal:

The Reverend gentleman wants to be helpful in case of attack. I say nothing. When we arrived in Aqua-Dulce-Sweetwater (a midway

point between Trinidad and Sweetwater) all at the place were pre-
pared to fight the gang and leader, if attacked. Possibly my silence
was construed as being ignorant of what the gang was capable of
doing. Whatever may have been the thoughts of those prepared to
defend their lives, we were not molested.

Sister Blandina's affection for Santa Fe was immediate. The
mountains surrounding the village reminded her of Italy. She was
moved by the history of the area, the churches, the cobbled streets,
and the statues of the saints that had been martyred. The satisfying
setting sparked her desire to resume her teaching duties. She was
escorted to the school by another nun and asked to consider how she
could improve the facility. In a journal entry dated March 1877, she
described the scene to her sister:

There were no black-boards, charts, maps, desks, books—nothing but
the teacher and the orphans. I said there were no books, but there
were two text books, one for the teacher, the other for the pupils! The
teacher was doing her best under such conditions. I made my report.
We need school supplies but was told we have no money to pay for
them; we have barely enough to purchase what is absolutely neces-
sary for existence.

Sister Blandina suggested that a request needed to be made
to the school board for help. "If they will give us a teacher's salary
we can use it to pay for the supplies," she reasoned. The sister was
informed that the board had been approached before, but that as the
pupils were residents, they couldn't allow a salary. Sister Blandina
asked if she could talk with them herself. News of the work she had
done with the school in Trinidad had reached the chairman of the

school board, and he was delighted to hear her out on the subject of a teacher's salary. He agreed to secure the funds if outside students were allowed to enroll. Sister Blandina agreed, and school supplies were ordered that same day. She then contacted people she had known in Colorado and asked them to lend support for the school. Within days the floors of the building were being repaired and pulleys and ropes for windows were installed, as well as blackboards.

Before the first semester started, Sister Blandina returned to Trinidad to visit her sister, who had been transferred west from the convent in Ohio. On her trip back to Santa Fe, news that Billy the Kid was ambushing stagecoaches sent a wave of panic over the stage driver and passengers. Nearly everyone aboard was cleaning and loading revolvers and rifles in anticipation of an assault.

The stage made a necessary stop midway through the journey. As Sister Blandina relayed in her journal:

> *It was here, that I proposed to Sister (a second nun on the trip) that we pray our beads out in the open plain, walking up and down some distance from the house . . . We started out again . . . about an hour or so later, the jockey sent his first message of alarm into the carriage.*
>
> *"There's something skimming over the plains, coming this way. . . ."*
>
> *"I would suggest putting revolvers out of sight," I told them. They looked at me as if to say that a woman is incapable of realizing extreme danger.*

A number of fast riders from every side caught up with the stage. One rider led the others to the site. Seeing who the man was, Sister Blandina shifted the bonnet on her head so the two could look into each other's eyes. It was Billy the Kid. He recognized her at once and "raised his large-brimmed hat with a wave and a bow," Sister Blandina remembered. "Before turning and riding away, he stopped to give us some of his wonderful antics on bronco maneuvers."

Sister Blandina's time teaching in Santa Fe was rewarding, and she took on more than just educating the class on the basics—she was also a music instructor. Using a donated piano and organ, the sister taught students to read music and prepared them for end-of-year programs.

In June 1878 she was called upon by the church to start work on a trade school for young women. As before, there was no money for such a venture. She was encouraged to do as she had done in Trinidad. Sister Blandina appealed to a talented artist named Projectus Mouly to assist her in developing a plan to meet the objective. As she recalled in her journal:

> *I told him my thoughts for building an Industrial School. The plans are out of all proportions to any building here, and far away from the imagination of the present population of Santa Fe. Keep in mind the fact that the inhabitants of the territory are still on terms of enmity with the Apaches and Navajos, and any railroad is yet three hundred and some miles from here.*
>
> *Was it the extreme pressure of mental distress being experienced by this young genius, or his determination to get away from what he believed would be his ultimate downfall, or my enthusiasm in plunging into a great undertaking requiring large sums of money and not a cent on hand, that made him say:*
>
> *"I'm with you, Sister, when do you wish to begin?"*

Sister Blandina consulted with the rector of the cathedral, and he gave her his blessing. He felt that the training school was greatly needed in the area.

"How much money have you to begin with, Sister?" he asked at the conclusion of their meeting.

"Not a cent, Father," she replied.

"And you want to build a three-story house in a country where there is not a mill, not a brickyard, nor a quarry of your own, nor limekilns, and, worse of all, not a cent on hand! Yet you want to begin to dig the foundation Monday morning. Do you know what some of us will say of you?" the Rector inquired.

Sister Blandina told him that she could guess what people would say, but was positive if given the chance she could begin the work right away.

"Let me hear, Sister, what you wish me to do?" he asked.

"Simply announce at the next Sunday Masses that the Sisters of Charity wish to build a house where girls in need can be trained in industries by which they can make a livelihood. Please say that our present wish is that a number of peons be paid by those disposed to do so, and sent to our front grounds to work on Monday and continue daily until the foundations are laid, each man to bring pick and shovel."

The Rector agreed to make the announcement, but did not believe that any men would come. The day after the plea was made from the pulpit twelve men arrived at the site of the school. The foundation was set and the building began soon after.

While Sister Blandina was busy teaching and overseeing the building of the schools, hospitals, and orphanages, Billy the Kid was busy terrorizing the countryside. She continued to pray for his soul and that he would have a chance to "reconcile his misdeeds with God before he was captured and killed."

When he finally met his demise in the summer of 1881, the sister lamented his passing. She wrote in her journal, "Poor, poor Billy the Kid was shot by Sheriff Patrick F. Garrett of Lincoln County. That ends the career of one who began his downward course at the age of twelve years by taking revenge for the insult that had been offered to his mother. Only now have I learned his proper name—William H. Bonney."

In August 1881, Sister Blandina was directed to move to Albuquerque. Over the ten-year period she lived there, she helped build three schools, including a school for Indians, and a mission. She saw the Wild West evolve from an untamed frontier to a civilized country, and she anticipated even greater changes as time went on. As she shared in her memoirs:

> *What was sandbanks and adobe houses has been transformed into green fields and stone buildings.. The transition period will cause many to forget the end of man's creation. When the sane period comes, there will be a further clearing up of mad house activities. The conscientious and level headed will emerge serene. The dishonest will fear exposure, the unsophisticated will be submerged, and the Catholic missionary apprehensive and on the alert to prevent wolves in sheep's clothing from entering the flock.*

Not everyone welcomed the changes the West was undergoing. Among those who fought the transformation were the Apache people, specifically, Chief Geronimo and his captain Victorio. Sister Blandina's journal contained a few entries about the fierce Indian leader and the impact he was having on the white men and women residing in the San Bernardino mountains and around Santa Fe. The sister empathized with Geronimo and the Native Americans that were being displaced. On February 2, 1886, she wrote:

> *The Apaches are leading our soldiers on a fine chase. Not only is Geronimo riding at large, but Victorio and other captains also. Last*

week Sister Catherine and myself visited one of the grading camps and stood on a mound where, the day before Victorio had scalped two of the working men. Everyone in the camp was as quiet as though nothing had occurred.

Now that the warriors of the Apache tribe have broken their Reservations, it is the general opinion that Geronimo will not stop his depredations until he is captured, dead or alive.

Poor savage beasts! How overflowing with injury and anger! Away from their Reservation, they still feel the atmosphere is theirs to breathe. Company after company of our soldiers are following the Apache's trail. What our government wants most is to capture Chief Geronimo. As the Apaches know this is their last chance for war, it will be some time before the tribe submits—at all events, not until Geronimo and his warriors are captured . . .

I have often compared what the secreted feelings and thoughts of Indians and the congenitally deaf must be like. That impression remains until an overpowering one removes the first, and it is the last impression which causes unlooked for consequences. The congenitally deaf have much in their favor, being surrounded by some care and culture which, to some extent, react toward the good, while the Indian has naught but savagery to influence them.

It was because of Sister Blandina's sympathy for the Indian's plight that she agreed to teach the Apache women and children in the area to read and write.

"To go to the Apaches would be the height of my earthly happiness," she recorded in her memoirs.

Sister Blandina's interest in education extended beyond the students she was assigned to teach. She worked closely with the superintendent and board members of the public schools to improve methods of teaching and petitioned lawmakers to pass bills legalizing school warrants. Warrants, or bonds, had been issued, but tax money was not being collected to pay for school upgrades, text books, and supplies. Her staunch position on the subject convinced political hopefuls to approve the bill.

On August 11, 1889, the Catholic Church recalled Sister Blandina to Trinidad and sent her sister to take over her job at Albuquerque. A dispute had erupted between the Colorado school board and the nuns who taught at the facility. The sisters were being asked to lay aside their religious garb. Sister Blandina was called upon to settle the matter and conduct the first teacher's public examination in the territory. The result of the examination was that four teachers Sister Blandina knew were ranked among the top educators in the West.

According to Sister Blandina's journal, the school board–meeting where the matter of the nuns' habits was discussed was a bit more volatile. The teachers' qualifications were not being called into question. The school board's position was that anything in a public school that even hinted of sectarianism would bring trouble and be indirectly in opposition to all the school laws.

"Summer of 1892," Sister Blandina's journal entry began, "the intent of the meeting was to notify me that 'under no circumstances does the school board want to lose our services, but we ask you to change your mode of dress.'

"I looked steadily at the chairman and replied: The Constitution of the United States gives me the same privilege to wear this mode of dress as it gives you to wear your trousers. Goodbye. . . ."

Her strong feelings on the matter did not sway the board from its objective. Sister Blandina lost that particular battle and was sent back to Albuquerque to supervise construction on a new hospital.

Sister Blandina returned to the motherhouse in Cincinnati, Ohio, in 1897 and worked with children, teaching and assisting attorneys in juvenile court cases. She also worked with Italian immigrant children. She and her sister established the Italian Welfare Center, which helped house the homeless and provide all in need with food and clothing.

In the winter of 1941, Sister Blandina was hospitalized with complications stemming from a broken hip. She died on February 23, 1941, a month after celebrating her ninety-first birthday. Many of her former students attended her funeral and remembered the purpose she lived by, "to teach and meet emergencies" as she saw them.

Mary Graves Clarke

The Sorrowful Teacher

"Mary Ann Graves was a lovely girl, of tall and slender build, and exceptionally beautiful carriage. Her features, her regularity, were of classic Grecian mould. Her eyes were dark, bright, and expressive."

—Historian and author Charles McGlashan, 1880

M ary Graves Clarke, a dark-haired woman with a pale face and deep age lines marking her high cheekbones and small mouth, sat behind a wooden desk staring out a window that was slightly tinged around the edges with frost. The view of the distant snow-covered mountains that loomed over Huntington Lake in Tulare County held her attention for a long while.

The eleven students in the one-room schoolhouse where Mary taught pored over the books in their laps, quietly waiting for their teacher to address them. The pupils ranged in age from six to fifteen years. The majority of the class was girls, a few of whom couldn't help themselves from whispering while casting worried glances at their distracted teacher. Finally, one of the children asked, "Mrs. Clarke, are you all right?"

Mary slowly turned to the pupils and nodded. "I'm fine," she assured them. "I was just remembering."

According to the journal kept by one of Mary's students, her "expression was one of sadness." In spite of her melancholy spirit she

*Photo of Mary Graves, reprinted from "History of the Donner Party"
by C.F. McGlashan*

led the students through a series of lessons then dismissed them for
recess. She followed them outside and for a moment was content
simply to watch them play. A cool breeze drew her attention back to
the mountains and drove her thoughts back to a time when she was
a teenager, hopeful and happy.

If she had stayed in Indiana where she was born on November 1, 1826, she might have married the boy next door, taught students to read and write at a schoolhouse in her hometown, and lived out her days watching her children and grandchildren grow up on the family farm. Her life, however, took a different course when her family joined the Donner Party in 1846 and headed west.

Mary was nineteen when her father, Franklin, made the decision to move his family to California. The Graveses joined a wagon train organized by George and Jacob Donner and James Reed and their families. The initial group set out from Springfield, Illinois, in April and was joined by additional members when it reached Independence, Missouri. Franklin and Elizabeth Graves and their nine children joined the Donner Party in August at Fort Bridger, Wyoming, with their belongings piled in three large wagons.

Mary was excited about the journey. She had no doubt heard stories of the golden land of opportunity and couldn't wait to see its riches for herself. She knew her family might experience difficulties getting there but that had not put a damper on her gleeful spirit. She didn't care that the trail was treacherous, and she wasn't afraid of the Indians that guarded the way. She placed all her faith in God and her father to get her and her family to their new home safely.

Historical records note that Mary was a beautiful young lady with dark eyes and long, wavy black hair. She carried her slender, five-foot, seven-inch frame with grace. Her complexion was creamy olive. She captured the attention of many of the twenty-two single men in the party, but she was engaged to John Snyder, the driver of one of her father's teams.

On October 5, 1846, Snyder and Milton Elliott, another driver, exchanged heated words over whose team of oxen could pull a load faster and raced each other to the top of the hill. When their teams got tangled up, Snyder became furious and started cussing at Elliott and beating his livestock with a whip-stock. Reed stepped in and tried to calm him down. Snyder thought Reed was threatening him, and he jumped off his wagon and beat Reed over the head with the butt end of his heavy whip-stock while Mary looked on in horror. When Reed managed to stand up and wipe the blood from his eyes, his wife ran over to help him, and Snyder hit her over the head too. Reed quickly pulled out a knife and stabbed him. Mary's intended died fifteen minutes later. The stunned onlookers were outraged. They wanted to hang Reed. Mary was asked to sit in judgment of him, but she refused. Reed was banished from the group.

The gleam in Mary's eyes had started to fade. The journey west was grueling. In addition to having battled the heat and rough terrain, the party had taken a "shortcut" to California that actually took them several hundred miles out of their way. Lack of water and a variety of petty arguments, like the one between Snyder, Elliott, and Reed, created strife among the party members. Their food was running low, and many of their oxen and horses had been stolen by Indians.

Mary and the others finally reached the Sierra Nevada mountains on October 28, 1856. Generally, this final pass brought joy to weary emigrants. But it brought terror and dismay to the Donner Party. They could see dark skies ahead. Soon the winter storm clouds dumped six inches of snow on the travelers. They were trapped; the snow prevented them from going any further.

The emigrants quickly built crude cabins near a lake to protect them from the cold. Mary's family shared their tiny makeshift home with another large family in the party. Food was scarce. Time passed and the snow continued to fall.

By mid-December, Mary, her father, and Charles Stanton realized they would have to organize a team and go for help. Fifteen members of the group, including Mary, her father, her sister, her brother-in-law, and two Indian guides, volunteered to be a part of the party and make their way over the summit to Sutter's Fort.

Wearing snowshoes made from oxbows and cowhide and carrying enough provisions to last them six days, the "Forlorn Hope" party set off. They soon encountered snowdrifts that varied in depth from twelve to sixty feet. Mary Graves trudged through the thick blanket of white with all the strength she had. In a December 1846 diary entry, she wrote:

> *We had a very slavish day's travel, climbing the divide. Nothing of interest occurred until reaching the summit.*
>
> *The scenery was too grand for me to pass without notice, the changes being so great; walking now on loose snow, and stepping on hard, slick rock a number of hundred yards in length. Being a little in the rear of the party, I had a chance to observe the company ahead, trudging along with packs on their back. It reminded me of some Norwegian fur company among the icebergs. I do remember a remark one of the company made here, that we were about as near heaven as we could get.*

Generally, the fifteen traveled without saying a word, their eyes fixed on the ground. The fatigue and dazzling sunlight made some of them, such as Charles Stanton, snow-blind. Every day, Charles fell further and further behind the others. On the third day, Charles staggered into camp long after the others had finished their meager meal. He never complained but struggled daily to keep pace with the others. Mary's heart broke for him.

On the fifth morning, the members of the Forlorn Hope set out, leaving Charles behind at the smoldering campfire, smoking a cigarette. Mary was worried; she ran back to Charles and asked him if he was coming. "Yes," he replied. "I am coming soon." All day long Mary kept looking back to see if Charles had caught up with the party. By the day's end, she knew he wasn't coming. Indeed, Charles Stanton had died.

Mary's father and two other men were the next to die. Before Franklin Graves passed away, he called his daughters to his side.

"You have to do whatever you can to stay alive. Think of your mother and brothers and sisters in the cabin at the lake. If you don't make it to Sutter's Fort, and send help, everyone at the lake will die. I want you to do what you have to. . . . Use my flesh to stay alive."

The mere thought of doing such a thing made the girls cry, but they knew he was right. They would have to resort to cannibalism to survive.

The remaining eleven members of the Forlorn Hope party sat down in the snow to discuss plans. Mary described in her diary what the party talked about:

We held a consultation, whether to go ahead without provisions, or go back to the cabins, where we must undoubtedly starve. Some of those who had children and families wished to go back, but the two Indians said they would go on to Captain Sutter's. I told them I would go too, for to go back and hear the cries of hunger from my little brothers and sisters was more than I could stand. I would go as far as I could, let the consequences be what they might.

As the party continued on together, another furious storm bombarded the Sierras.

More men died and the women were weakening. It had been twelve days since the rescue team had left their loved ones and friends at the cabins. They had walked so many miles that their feet were bleeding. They were starving and cold. Mary's diary described the horror she endured:

Our only chance for campfire for the night was to hunt a dead tree of some description, and set fire to it. The hemlock being the best and generally the largest timber, it was our custom to select the driest we could find without leaving our course.

When the fire would reach the top of the tree, the falling limbs would fall all around us and bury themselves in the snow, but we heeded them not. Sometimes the falling, blazing limbs would brush our clothes, but they never hit us; that would have been too lucky a hit. We would sit or lie on the snow, and rest our weary frames. We would sleep, only to dream of something nice to eat, and awake again to disappointment. Such was our sad fate.

One morning Mary and a man named William Eddy struck out on their own to find food. They had gone two miles when they noticed a place where a deer had slept the night before. The two burst into tears at the hope of finding the animal. They dropped to their knees to pray. When they sighted the buck, William fired his rifle at it. The deer continued running.

Mary cried out, "Oh dear God, you have missed it." The deer suddenly dropped down in the snow and the pair raced toward it. William cut a deep V in its throat, and the two fell on the animal and drank the warm blood.

Within a few days there was nothing left of the deer, and starvation again set in. Only five women and two men still remained. The feeble party traveled on day after day. Their strength was almost gone when someone noticed tracks in the snow.

"It was human tracks," Mary later said. "Can anyone imagine the joy those footprints gave us? We ran as fast as our strength would carry us."

The group followed the tracks until they came in full view of a Washo Indian camp. The Indian women and children stared in amazement at the skeleton-like figures that came into their camp. They quickly fed the starving group and tended to their battered feet and other wounds. It had been thirty-two days since the party had left the lake.

Mary Graves no longer looked like she did when the journey began. Her high cheekbones were grotesquely prominent and her cheeks were buried deep below them. Her eyes were dim and sunken. Her once-perfect skin now had the appearance of baked leather. With good food and much care, her looks would be restored, but her spirit would never be the same.

She had endured a hard trek over the pass to get help for her family and the other starving emigrants, but all she could think about was making sure those back at the lake were saved.

Relief parties from Sutter's Fort rescued Mary's family and the rest of the surviving members of the Donner Party in April. Mary's mother and five-year-old brother had died. Mary and her sister, Sarah, were now in charge of their younger siblings.

The forty-six remaining members of the party were escorted to Sutter's Fort. The horrific tales of survival they relayed to the inquisitive people who gathered around them brought tears to their eyes. Mary's once cheerful disposition had now been replaced with a despondent nature. She thrived on the stories told about her mother in her last days. Mary's mother was praised by the survivors for her charity. She was a generous woman who gave all she had to give. Mary was inspired by her mother's actions, and it spurred her on despite her depression.

On May 16, 1847, Mary married Edward Pyle, a member of the relief expedition that went to the aid of the Donner Party. The couple left Sutter's Fort with her brother and sisters and settled in the San Jose area. It was here that she entered the teaching profession. Her career was interrupted when Edward disappeared shortly after they arrived. Mary's search for her husband ended after a year when his murdered body was discovered.

Antonio Valencia was tried and convicted for the crime. Valencia had dragged Edward one hundred yards at the end of his rope and then cut his throat. His body was shot full of arrows to give the impression that death was the result of an Indian attack.

Valencia was sentenced to be hanged, and Mary was determined that justice would be served. On the off chance a vigilante group would try to kill him, either by poisoning or shooting him before the execution date, Mary went to the prison every day and prepared the murderer's meals.

In 1852 Mary married a sheep rancher named J. T. Clarke and they moved to a town near the White River in Tulare County. She became the region's first schoolteacher, educating generations of children including the six she and J. T. had.

Mary always stayed close to her home. Other members of the Donner Party eventually returned to the "place of horror" as Mary called it, but she never did. Her students and family often caught her staring regretfully out over the Sierra mountain range. All she wanted to do was forget the tragedy. It was something her children and grandchildren remembered was impossible for her to do.

Mary Ann Graves Pyle Clarke died of pneumonia in Traver, Tulare County, on March 9, 1891. Her twenty-six-year-old son had been struggling with the same ailment for several days. He passed away four days prior to his mother. Mary was sixty-five years old when she died.

Eliza Mott

The Carson Valley Teacher

*"I seldom if ever saw a more beaming face . . .she did all the good that she could in
every way she could wherever and to whomever she could."*

—Reverend Francis C. Ball recollection
of Eliza at her funeral, 1909

A precocious, wide-eyed seven-year-old boy studied a sample
of the alphabet in front of him and tried to copy the material
onto a small slate with a broken piece of chalk. His teacher, Mrs.
Eliza Mott, stood over his shoulder, kindly guiding him through the
work and praising him for his effort. A handful of other youngsters
reviewed the letters and practiced writing them out with pencil stubs
on scraps of paper. Eliza's kitchen served as a classroom, and students
sat on bare logs around a crude, wooden table—some enjoying the
learning process; others cursing the day school was created.

The Carson Valley area where Eliza and her husband, Israel, settled in 1851 needed a place where children could learn the three R's.
In early 1852, the Motts offered their home as a temporary school;
and, armed with a pair of McGuffey Readers, Eliza began teaching. Monday through Friday she welcomed boys and girls dressed in
plaid, gingham dresses, home-knit stockings, tan trousers and over-
shirts, who were either barefoot or wearing rough shoes with hard
leather soles. The class ranged in age from five to eleven years. It

toiled over a variety of subjects, sharing the limited books on spelling and arithmetic. On a few occasions, Eliza escorted the children to the small cemetery to read the epitaphs on the tombstones. It served not only to aid the students in learning to read but instilled a sense of reverence for those who had passed away helping to tame the wild territory.

In addition to their studies, Eliza had her students cut the wood for the fire, bring in water, sweep the floor, and keep the room tidy. She considered it important to teach her pupils responsibility for their classroom as well as the basic fundamentals of reading, spelling, history, and geography.

Eliza Ann Middaugh was born on January 13, 1829, in Toronto, Canada. Her family moved to Lee County, Iowa, in 1842, and it was there she developed her teaching skills. She excelled at school and aspired to make great strides in the field of education.

She met and fell in love with Israel Mott when she was twenty-one years old and the two were married on April 10, 1850.

Like thousands of other pioneers of that time, Israel and Eliza emigrated west in search of a utopian-style life. In early 1851 the newlyweds completed the first leg of their journey in Salt Lake City. Among the belongings that Eliza had had transported from Iowa and that were still intact were a cherry-wood piano and a rocking chair. Shortly after they arrived in Utah, Eliza gave birth to the first of the four children she and Israel would have together. When she was ready to travel again, the Motts joined a Mormon wagon train and headed toward California.

Kit Carson, the famed American frontiersman, led the party, which consisted of more than thirty men and eighteen women. The caravan stopped at Mormon Station in northern Nevada on July 14, 1851. After putting new shoes on the oxen and loading provisions onto their tattered Conestoga wagon, Israel decided he liked the region too much to continue on. He escorted his wife and child to a suitable spot south along the Carson River route and claimed a twenty-one-hundred-acre section of land as his own.

Using abandoned wagon beds, Israel built a house for his family next to a stream at the base of the Sierra Nevada Mountains. According to historical journals, "he made a window sash with a jack-knife and paid seventy-five cents for a seven-by-nine inch window glass to put into it." The Motts were the first white settlers to build a home in the valley, and Eliza was its first woman settler.

The need for a school became apparent as more settlers moved into Carson Valley. Many of the pioneers who had arrived were members of Israel's extended family—his parents, brothers, sisters, aunts, and uncles. By 1854 the area was known as Mottsville, and among Eliza's first students at the Mottsville School were her own children as well as her nieces and nephews.

Eliza's duties at the homestead were extensive and had to be maintained even though she taught school. An average day began before dawn. She would tend to her two children, milk six or seven cows, and then return to cook breakfast for her family and hired hands. Next she prepared lunches for the students and then started preparing for school. Eliza eventually hired a teacher named Ms. Allen to help her with the lessons and the influx of new pupils.

By the fall term of 1855, the Mottsville School had officially outgrown Eliza's kitchen. In early 1856 a schoolhouse was built with plastered walls and six-pane windows. An educator from the East was employed as the schoolmaster, and Eliza resigned as teacher to care for her family full time.

On November 11, 1856, Eliza and Israel had their third child, a daughter. She died three months after she was born, and they buried the infant in the backyard of the Mott home. Not long after her passing, a neighbor's child died and was buried there as well. These two graves marked the place that subsequently became the official Mottsville Cemetery.

The Motts dedicated themselves to their homestead and to serving the community. Israel became one of the first judges of the election in the Mottsville precinct, and the first court was held in Israel and Eliza's barn. Eliza maintained a garden, raising vegetables for her family and needy neighbors. She made clothes for the poor and was oftentimes called on to assist with the delivery of a baby or help with a sick child.

In time Eliza and Israel had two more children. In total they had two boys and two girls. Israel died suddenly in 1864, leaving Eliza alone to raise their offspring and maintain the ranch. A. M. Taylor, a friend and neighbor, helped Eliza and her children with chores, and they eventually fell in love. A. M. and Eliza wed on November 15, 1864, and together they operated her portion of the Mott family claim.

The couple decided to raise pigs on the farm as well as continuing on with the prosperous milk-cow venture. Eliza made a variety of products using the milk from their herd. She would set milk in big pans every morning, and later she would skim off the cream to make butter and cheese. After it was churned and placed in molds, it was taken to Carson City to be sold.

A. M. Taylor died on November 14, 1890, and Eliza then depended on her sons to care for her. In her later years she was plagued with chronic pain from a bad tooth. Rather than have it pulled, she suffered through by smoking a pipe or a cigar. She insisted that the smoke brought her some relief.

Mrs. Mott-Taylor passed away in January 1909. Her funeral was appropriately held at the Mottsville schoolhouse, the institution she had founded. Rev. Francis C. Ball delivered Eliza's eulogy. He spoke in glowing terms about her life and legacy. She was remembered as a woman "whose kind acts were done out of the pure goodness of her heart without thought or hope of reward."

According to a Carson Valley newspaper, *Genoa Weekly Courier,* "a very large procession accompanied the remains to the Mottsville Cemetery near where she settled in those far-off, rigorous pioneer days, and there at the base of God's most majestic mountains, the Sierras, all that was mortal of this good woman, Mrs. Eliza Mott-Taylor, was tenderly laid to rest."

Anna Webber

The Prairie Teacher

"I'm not really settled to school teaching yet because I expect more scholars and new furniture. I hope it will come soon, for it seems almost impossible to get along with nothing to write on, or no place to put books."

—ANNA WEBBER'S ASSESSMENT OF HER CLASSROOM TWELVE
WEEKS AFTER SCHOOL HAD STARTED, MAY 13, 1881

Twenty-one-year-old Anna Webber rubbed her eyes and leaned against the rough wall of the sod schoolhouse where she taught. The view from the window of the small building framed the tall grass and wheat fields around Blue Hill, Kansas, perfectly. A slight breeze in the middle distance brushed across the tops of cottonwood trees lining the banks of the Solomon River, richly adding to the peaceful scene.

Anna squinted into the sunlight filtering into the tiny classroom and stretched her arms over her head. The one-room schoolhouse was empty of students, and the young teacher was sitting on the floor grading papers. The room was only big enough for a half a dozen pupils but served more than sixteen children on most days.

Inside the roughly constructed building, made from strips cut from the prairie earth found in abundance around the small settlement, the furnishings consisted of a chair for the teacher and several boards balanced on rocks for the students to sit on. There was no blackboard and no writing desks. The primitive conditions made Anna's job more difficult than she had anticipated and robbed her of the joy she initially felt when she entered the profession.

The town in Mitchell County, Kansas, where Anna held her first teaching assignment in 1881, was a growing community of farmers and railroad workers. Five years before her arrival, the area had been ravaged by hordes of grasshoppers. The insects destroyed crops and drove settlers away for a time. The ever-advancing railroad brought many back to the fertile ground to raise corn, wheat, and rye. Anna's family was among the people who returned to the region to start life anew.

Anna Webber was born in Breckenridge, Kansas, on September 16, 1860. Her parents, William Ellsworth and Thankful Delila Webber, relocated to Iowa shortly after she arrived and remained there until Thankful's untimely death in 1872. Anna's father remarried and moved his new wife and children back to Kansas the following year. Little is known of Anna's youth. Historical records note that she attended school in Mitchell County and in the spring of 1881 took and passed her teacher's examination.

Eleven boys and five girls were enrolled when Anna began her first day at Blue Hill school. The students ranged in age from six to thirteen years, and the school term was three months long.

Anna kept a journal during her time on the job. The daily entries describe the expansive landscape and weather, her students, and the tasks at hand. Selections from her diary appear just as she wrote them more than one hundred and twenty-five years ago:

MONDAY, MAY 9, 1881. Well, here I am at my first school. I realy wander if I'll like it. I arrived at the house about eight o'clock. It is a very pleasant looking place. I wander how I'll get along. My antici-pations are great—I am going to try to make rapid improvement. I hope the next three months will not be lost. And I trust they will not be if I continue with the effort I've made today. There is something in which I am bound to improve, and that is in speaking low (tho it is as natural for me, as it is to see). The Supt gave me such a desperate look while I was reading at the examination, that I resolved to "learn to read loud." I think if hollowing will do any good I'll overcome that fault entirely. I have a scholar that is some deaf, and I've "hollered" and talked today until my throat aches.

I am among entire strangers, not knowing before I came here a single person.

THURSDAY, MAY 12. It has been dark and cloudy, but cool and suitable to study. I am getting along splendidly. Now if I only had seats and a black board, it would be so nice. I know I am improving, and think the scholars are. I have not such a school as I wanted, but I'll do the best I can. Well I'll have to go down and get Mrs. McPeak's broom, and sweep the school-house.

FRIDAY, MAY 20, 1881. O, Dear! Almost two weeks of my school gone. And how do I like teaching by this time? Well, I hardly know. I think I like it. I know I would like it better if things were different. As it is I do not make the progress I had [expected] to. About all I learn is in studying after school is out. And then I am so tired and figety, I can do nothing scarcely, unless it is to walk about, or go to sleep. perhaps that will wear off tho' as I get more used to teaching. If I only had large scholars that were farther advanced, I would like it.

But I haven't so I'll have to make the best of it. If I can get to Beloit I will get me a grammar, and some kind of a writing system. But I am so far from town that I don't expect to get there until after school is out. You can't get your mail here, or get a letter to the office—any to often. I have a letter now I should like to send to the

*office, but I guess that is all the good it will do me. And I want some
ink, yes and something to write on. Before I began school I thought
I would write an Essay every day, and I haven't written one yet,—
but I must try, it will be a failure I expect, but I can't do more than
fail though. I guess I'll take Nature as the subject. It seems as if there
is enough to write on that. I am surrounded by nature, about all I
see is the hills, and all I hear is the noise of the birds, and a dozen or
more of children.*

*TUESDAY, MAY 24. I have had rather a dull school today, or
it seems that way to me. Perhaps it is because I have had so much
trouble with Charlie A. It seems impossibility for him to learn the
alphabet. He is such a careless, lazy little rascal. He seems to take no
interest whatever in trying to learn. I don't know what to do with
him. A little boy came to visit our school this afternoon.*

*I do wish those seats would come! They are not going after them
now until they get their corn planted. Then perhaps it will be, "not
till after harvest," and I wouldn't wonder if by that time it would be
"Let's build a good house first." Nothing extraordinary has happened
in school today.*

*MONDAY, MAY 30, 1881. School-day has arrived again. And
I have six new scholars. It makes my school nearly twice as before.
But the best is, they have brought a table for us to use. They did not
get the seats Friday. The table makes it seem like a different place. I
feel real tired tonight, something like I did the evening after my first
day's experience. I was very busy this forenoon. So busy that I did
not have spare time to turn around in. Did not get through until a
quarter past twelve, but got things so I [will] not be in a "rush" this
afternoon. I spent a disagreeable day pleasantly yesterday. I wrote a
letter to Nellie in the forenoon, and spent the afternoon in reading. I*

did intend to attend Quarterly Meeting, but it rained so as to make that impossible. Saturday I had laid off as a day of general study. But I studied very little, I did a little sewing, and that was about all I did do.

SATURDAY, JUNE 4, 1881. I am teaching today. I have only eight scholars. The wind is blowing real hard, and it is quite warm. Bro. Birch called on us this morning. I feel to mean for any use today. I believe I have not studied a bit today. Just the minute I sit down I go to sleep. I have a dull, dizzy head-ache, I don't know whether it is sickness, or pure laziness. I wonder where I will be one month from today. I have to go down and iron this evening.

WEDNESDAY, JUNE 8. It is nearly sundown. I have been writing for an hour and a half. I am nearly starved. I had the misfortune to have to keep a scholar after school today. The little chap blacked his face in school-time, and made a real jubilee.—I don't like to punish a pupil, and I have very little of it to do. They all try to do right. And study well. Once in a while one of them takes a contrary spell, but they soon get over it and are as good as can be.

THURSDAY, JUNE 9. It looks like we were going to get a terriable storm tonight, And it will storm before I can get home if I don't go. (Friday.)

And I did go, not waiting even to straighten the schoolhouse. [One sheet of the diary is missing.] had a pleasant time. The pupils have had pretty good lessons, and been quiet. Frank B. came, but has been real sick, he looks bad. There are so many little funny things happen in school. I cannot keep from laughing, sometimes when I know I ought not to. I do wish I could take music lessons, if I had money I would take them. It is like school teaching. I always wanted to teach, and wanted to learn music, but I am afraid like the school-teaching, it will be so long before I get the opportunity, and I will have been so often disgusted, and out of patients with my efforts, that when the time comes (if it ever does,) it will have lost half the charms.

TUESDAY, JUNE 21. Another day of school has gone, Another rather hard one, to. I cannot think of any thing to write. I have not got entirely over my chagrin yet. Nothing unusual has happened in school today. We had a nice rain last night, that cooled the atmosphere and made it more pleasant for studying. There was a real wind storm and I expected the schoolhouse would be among the missing, but it was not.

WEDNESDAY, JUNE 22. Today finishes the seventh week of my school. There are five more yet. It is getting monotonous. not the school, but the surroundings, just the same quietness, seeing the same objects, and going through the same performances day after day, with no merriment or changes mix in it. How I dread to see the fourth come. I don't know whether I'll get to go home, or have to stay here, or get to go any place. I don't believe it does any good to think of it, things do about as they please in spite of me. Nothing has happened in school today.

THURSDAY, JULY 7. My Land! The wind blows hard enough to take a persons head off. I'll declare if I don't just dread these hot windy day[s]. We have had to keep the door shut most of the time today. I have only nine scholars now. The children are playing, and shake the house till I can't make a straight mark.

SATURDAY, JULY 16. There is only nine days more of school. It seems a long time since I left home, but it does not seem like I had taught nearly three months.

The school-house looks so nice that I hate to leave it. Well I have to go down and iron, or else make out the teachers report, this evening. I have had a pretty good school today.

FRIDAY, JULY 22. I have only four days more of school. it is cool and pleasant this morning. I am sorry school is so near out. Well I have to scrub the floor this evening, for there is preaching here Sunday. And I have to iron, and get ready for the picnic tomorrow. I had a nice school this forenoon, but it was not so pleasant this afternoon. I had to keep two scholars this evening, and that is not all I did for them, the little rascals. Well, if I dont hurry faster I won't get half my work done.

WEDNESDAY, JULY 27, 1881, HALF PAST SEVEN A. M. This is the last day. It dont seem that it is tho'. It dont seem like there is any thing unusual about it. it seems like a dark cloudy rainy school-day, and that is all.

HALF PAST FIVE, P. M. My school is out. It is all over and done with. And I am just a little glad, and considerable tired. I have been dreading it so long. It was not so hard after all. But there was not many here.

That made the difference. It was so "rainy" that they feared to come. We had a pretty nice time. But I cannot enjoy myself, or be lively now, it makes little difference where I am. I am going home tomorrow, and next week to school. Well school is out, I can think of nothing but that I should like to write more but have not time. Goodby old Diary.

Anna Webber continued to teach school in Blue Hills and two additional Kansas counties throughout the 1880s. She joined the staff of the Kansas Industrial School in June 1890 and was the head of the sewing department. That same year she met Robert H. Gravatt, and the two were married on February 5, 1891. Their daughter Lila followed in her mother's footsteps and became a prominent teacher of American history at Lincoln High School in Nebraska.

Tabitha Brown

The Grandmother Teacher

"I provided for myself a good ox wagon-team, a good supply of what was requisite for the comfort of myself, Captain Brown and my driver."

—TABITHA BROWN'S RECOLLECTION OF THE
PREPARATION FOR HER TRIP
OVERLAND TO OREGON, 1854

It seemed to pioneer Tabitha Brown that the entire East Coast population had converged on the frontier town of Independence, Missouri. Thousands of excited immigrants tended to their livestock and their wagon trains that were filled to overflowing before beginning the long journey across the plains west. The congested river city was the start of the Oregon Trail. Everywhere you looked, heavily laden mules wagged their large packs, bristling with shovels and picks. Teamsters led oxen and mule teams down the dusty thoroughfares pulling generations of families and supplies. All were giddy with the possibility of a prosperous life beyond the Rockies. Accompanied by her grandson, sixty-six-year-old Tabitha wove in and out of the busy storefronts and tent shops, watching merchants selling a variety of goods, from apples to moccasins.

Numerous blacksmiths all around pounded out shoes for a line of horses, and music from saloons drifted out into the street enticing people to step inside before heading off.

Tabitha Brown

As Tabitha marveled at the sites and sounds, she recalled visiting the area shortly after she and her now-deceased husband had married. The location had been a wilderness of solitude and silence then. Now prospectors, engineers, promoters, adventurers, gamblers, and soiled doves had flocked to the thriving hamlet. Two-story buildings had sprouted like wild weeds and cabins and churches followed suit.

In 1846 Tabitha decided to leave her home in Hickory Grove, Missouri, and move to Oregon. Her son Orus had returned from the lush Willamette Valley of the Northwest and convinced his mother and extended family to relocate. His enthusiasm for the farming opportunities there was infectious. Weighing one hundred pounds and dragging a partially paralyzed leg, Tabitha packed her belongings and eagerly looked forward to the move. She was a tenacious woman whose life in Missouri had been a mixture of heartbreak and joy.

Born on May 1, 1780, in Brimfield, Massachusetts, Tabitha was educated as a teacher and taught school for a few years before marrying the Reverend Clark Brown. The pair then moved to Missouri where Clark served as an Episcopalian preacher. The couple had three children: two boys they named Orus and Manthano, and a girl they called Pherne. After Rev. Brown died in 1817, Tabitha returned to the teaching profession to support her family.

Tabitha not only made the trip west with her son Orus, his wife, and their eight children, but traveled with her daughter, her husband, their five youngsters, and Tabitha's seventy-seven-year-old brother-in-law, former sea captain, John Brown. She made her way down the long trail with the help of a cane and periodically rested her weary frame in a rocking chair that was loaded and unloaded from the back of her wagon.

A gold prospector in 1849 noted in a letter home that "the overland journey is one of the most unfortunate undertakings to which man may allow himself to be lured, because he cannot possibly have any conception before starting of this kind of traveling." That was certainly the case for Tabitha and her family. In spite of the unforeseen obstacles and personal disabilities, the widow was determined to reach the spot her son called "Paradise." From the moment the party left Independence, Tabitha's excessively attentive family watched over the senior citizen. Although she preferred to do for herself, her children insisted on seeing to her every need.

Tabitha and Captain Brown's wagon was one of sixty in the train. To make traveling a little more manageable, the leader of the expedition divided the train into fifteen platoons of four wagons each. On the days Tabitha's platoon and wagon were in the lead she happily drank in the passing scenery. A cloud of dust created by her fellow sojourners' wagons obscured her view of the landscape when her vehicle rotated to the end of the caravan, however. An average day's travel was nine to ten hours long with an hour break at noon. Tabitha felt as though the trip was being rushed.

"Some people in this train have only one thing in mind," she noted in her memoirs. "They just want to push everybody to the limit to get to Oregon as fast as they can."

Her son explained that they had to hurry along to avoid heavy rains or unexpected snowstorms over mountain passes. She understood his reasoning but felt it was unlikely given the time of year they were traveling.

"When the oxen need rest and we're camped in a place with good grass and water, we ought to take advantage of it," she later wrote.

During the first leg of the journey, the emigrants crossed the Big Blue River in Kansas near Alcove Springs and then followed the Little Blue River into Nebraska. Tabitha spent part of the long drive watching her daughter sketch the sights, reading about the Oregon territory, and playing word games with her grandchildren. At times her wagon and a few others lagged behind the pilot vehicle to enjoy the scenery and rest. Orus eventually became too frustrated to continue on with those he believed were slowing the entire train down, and a decision was made to split the wagons up to make better time.

Orus and his family and twenty-nine other wagons were going to move on ahead after they reached a spot called Ash Hollow, three miles south of Lewellen, Nebraska. Ash Hollow was the steepest descent on the trail. The pioneers' belongings had to be tied to the wagons and the wagons lowered down the green embankment below. Everyone had to walk alongside the vehicles and the teams. Tabitha was required to do the same but realized soon after she started that she could not make it over the pass on foot. She agreed to be carried down the precipice by two of the strongest men in the party.

The elderly woman's knowledge of the rocks and plants on the route was educational for the children on the journey. She taught them the names of the various flowers and trees, and stony landmarks such as Chimney, Courthouse, and Jail Rocks. All three of the natural landmarks helped settlers find their way to their final destinations.

Tabitha found one of the most interesting trail markers to be Post Office Rock. The name of the site was etched into the granite ledges and contained a number of letters left behind from people in preceding trains. Some of the notes contained warnings for travelers continuing along the trail. "Upon leaving the North Platte area," the tattered notes read, "the journey gets difficult. Ahead is fifty miles of dry desert with only one good camping spot."

Tabitha and the others pressed on in spite of the hardships that lay ahead. The hot sun baked the wagon trail, and everyone who dared sit inside their canvas enclosures. The elderly Miss Brown plastered a smile of resolve on her face and urged her ox team through the loose sand. When the weight became too much for the animals to manage, nonessential items had to be unloaded from the wagon and deposited in the desert. Tabitha gave up her iron pots and pans, cooking utensils, and a carved walnut bedstand.

Lack of water was a hardship not only for the pioneers but for the livestock pulling the vehicles. They dragged their feet, panted, and bawled for refreshments.

"It was pitiful to hear," Tabitha wrote in her journal. "We couldn't wait to reach the Sweetwater River in southern Wyoming and relieve their agony."

When they arrived at the eighty-foot-wide body of water, they filled their canteens and water barrels and gave the animals a chance to replenish themselves. After only a day's rest, the wagon train moved on toward Independence Rock. The party made it to the most famous of all the Oregon Trail landmarks on July 4, 1846. Thousands of emigrants who had previously passed through the area had carved their names on the massive boulder. Tabitha referred to it as the "Great Register of the Desert," and with her permission her grandson proudly etched her name into the stone.

The wagon train pilot led Tabitha and the other travelers further down the trail through the granite walls of Devil's Gate where they began to steadily ascend the south pass of the Rockies. The precarious road was closely lined with emigrants.

By August 9, 1856, Tabitha and her fellow pioneers had traveled more than 1,400 miles. After passing the American Falls on the Snake River in Idaho, the group made camp and began discussing the next leg of the journey. They had been on the trial for more than three months, were extremely tired, and on more than one occasion, had been forced to abandon a portion of their belongings. Tensions were running high and most just wanted to get to their new home in the Willamette Valley quickly. The leaders of the group decided to venture off the well-established trail and pursue a cut-off promoted by a gentleman on the train named Jesse Applegate.

Applegate was a veteran traveler and assured the group that the new route he had discovered would get them to the settlement quicker than the traditional course. Applegate's route had many dangers associated with it—rugged terrain, the possibility of encountering bad weather, and warring natives who were upset by the encroaching presence of white men. Tabitha and many others agreed to take the trail.

Ninety-eight men, fifty women (including Tabitha), and several children were a part of the team that followed Applegate across northern Utah and Nevada and over the mountains of southern Oregon. The trip was grueling; at times they were on the move for forty-eight hours straight in order to make it through the desert.

Livestock, too weak to continue on, had to be left behind. Overgrown trails toppled and destroyed wagons. Indians killed some of the oxen and milk cows and drove off herds of beef cattle. Rain and hail storms drenched the roads and washed them out. Tabitha's brother-in-law's health began failing due to exhaustion and overexposure to the elements.

In addition to the other concerns for safety and lack of food, Tabitha worried that she wouldn't be able to make it to the camp in Oregon because of her age and fretted over the problem that it could pose if she too got sick. The loss of animals meant that more personal effects had to be left along the trail to assure that the remaining mules could haul the wagons. Tabitha finally parted with her rocking chair near the Rogue River. So many pack animals died that eventually several of the wagons had to be abandoned altogether. The pioneers were forced either to walk or ride one of the horses that was well enough to carry them.

"I rode through the Umpqua Mountains in three days at the risk of life, on horseback, having lost my wagon and all that I had but the horse I was on," she wrote.

Tabitha and John got separated from the train for a short while. John had fallen behind because he was ill, and Tabitha stayed with him to help. She managed to make a crude canvas lean-to in a copse of trees and guided John to the location where he could be protected from a pouring rain. The following morning the pair was found and reunited with their party.

The Applegate route proved to be more of a speculative roadway than a tried one. By the time Tabitha and the other settlers who had chosen to follow the so-called trailblazer reached the banks of the Willamette River in Oregon, they were out of food, their clothes and shoes were completely worn, and they were too weak to travel long periods of time. An advanced team had to be sent ahead to the settlement to secure provisions and bring them back to the cold, beleaguered group.

Tabitha and her fellow travelers finally made it to their destination on Christmas Day 1846. They arrived at a camp called Oregon City. Rain continued to pound the settlement, which consisted of three or four dozen dwellings, and everyone scrambled for a dry place to rest their weary frames. Tabitha sought protection from the elements at the home of a Methodist missionary.

"It was the first house I had set my feet in for nine months," she later wrote.

Once the sun had come out and Tabitha's family had an opportunity to set up tents and purchase provisions, they quickly sent for her. She was not willing to relocate, however. She had decided that no house would be large enough to hold her daughter or son's family, along with her and her brother-in-law.

"I've got to Oregon, as I intended to," she gently explained to her grandson. "But I've lost my wagon and all my possessions, except for what I have on my back and the little dab in my saddlebag. And there's Captain John to be looked after. He can't live out his life in a tent."

Although Tabitha's family objected, she insisted on looking for a job to provide for herself and Captain John. She'd hoped to acquire a position teaching, but in the interim took a job as a housekeeper for the Methodist missionary.

"I twiddled my thumbs all the way across the plains and let them make an old woman out of me," Tabitha penned in her journal. "But now I'm here and going to have my way for a change."

Tabitha's children moved to homesteads on the Tualatin Plains near the town of Salem and Willamette Falls. She visited whenever she could afford to do so. She enjoyed her work and looked forward to the day she could return to the field of education. A coin found in the fingertip of one of her gloves provided her with the financial incentive to realize her goal.

"What I supposed to be a button—was worth six and a quarter cents," Tabitha noted in her journal. "I bought three needles, traded some old clothes to Native women in return for buckskin and worked them into gloves for the Oregon ladies and gentlemen, which cleared me upwards of $30."

The funds made it possible for Tabitha eventually to accompany missionary Henry Clark and his family to Forest Grove, a town west of Tualatin, and take in orphan Indian children who needed a home and wanted to learn to read and write.

"He (Rev. Clark) proposed to . . . establish a school in the plains," Tabitha recalled in 1854. "I was to go into the log meeting house and receive all the children rich and poor, who wanted to learn."

Within the first year of starting the school and orphanage in March 1848, Tabitha had twelve children in her care. They used the church as both a classroom and home, but it was clear they needed more space.

"Mr. Clark fell trees and built a school and houses for teachers and visiting clergy," Tabitha remembered. "Those parents who were able to pay, were asked to contribute a $1 a week for board, tuition, washing, and all. I agreed to labor for one year for nothing, while Mr. Clark and others were to assist as far as they were able in furnishing provisions. Our students ranged in age from four years old to twenty-one years old."

The Tualatin Academy, as it came to be known, was chartered by the territorial legislature on September 26, 1849. In addition to their daily studies, students and residents helped maintain the grounds, did laundry, cooked, cleaned, and cared for the milk cows and chickens. Tabitha taught classes, oversaw all the domestic activities, lent support when needed, and settled any disputes that arose between the youngsters.

In the beginning the only book at the school was a Bible. Donations from local businesses made it possible for readers, spellers, math, and history books to be purchased. A missionary had brought two hundred such volumes to the territory by ship. The school grew both in the number of the students and in the buildings necessary to accommodate them. Seven years after Tabitha began teaching at the facility, the school's charter was amended to include the name of the outgrowth of the Tualatin Academy, the Pacific University.

Tabitha worked at the school for ten years. During that time she managed to save enough money to purchase her own home and eight other pieces of property in Forest Grove. When she died at the age of seventy-eight, she had more than $1,000 in cash. Five hundred dollars of the money she had saved was donated to the academy.

Although the academy closed in 1915, the university is still in existence. It has achieved high ratings in the category of private regional and liberal arts universities and is now best known for its College of Optometry.

Olive Mann Isbell

The Mission Teacher

"I have all that I want here, and what more could I have elsewhere? I have tried luxury without health, and a wild mountain life with it. Give me the latter, with the free air, the dashing streams, the swinging woods, the laughing flowers and the exulting birds."

—Olive Mann Isbell's thoughts about living
in California, November 14, 1849

Twenty-two-year-old Olive Isbell cradled a loaded rifle in her arms and scanned the hilly landscape surrounding the adobe school where she taught at the Santa Clara Mission in California. From far off she could hear a gun spit in swift five-syllable defiance, and she readied herself for a potential attack on the building. Twenty preoccupied students toiled away at the books and lessons in front of them. The exchange of gunfire was so routine it barely disturbed their studies.

The mission was under fire from the Mexican Army, which was trying to reclaim land it believed belonged to Mexico. Settlers scattered throughout the area had converged on the site for protection.

More than one hundred and ninety-five people with their wagon trains and pack animals spread out over various sections of the mission were busy loading weapons and preparing themselves for a fight. A number of those people had contracted typhoid fever.

Olive Mann Isbell

They were weak and at times unable to work, and they desperately needed medical attention.

Olive had gathered the healthy children together at a stable on the far side of the compound. It was her way of keeping the young-sters occupied and safe during the uprising. The one-room, makeshift schoolhouse was 15 feet square, thick with flies and fleas, with dirt floors and the stench of manure. A few crude tables and benches made from scraps of wood were used as desks and chairs for the pupils, who ranged in age from six to fourteen years old. A fire pit in the center of the room kept the class warm, and the smoke from the hearth escaped through a large hole in the roof.

The scant school supplies consisted of five McGuffey Readers, a half a dozen spellers, and three arithmetic and geography books. There were no pencils, pens, or paper. Olive used a long stick to scratch the alphabet into the dry ground. Her students practiced writing their letters with seared pieces of charcoal. Using the palms of their hands as slates they copied their A-B-Cs with the cool, black bits. Sarah Aram, one of Olive's students, vividly remembered later in her life the "look of the letter E printed on her hand."

Pupils at the Santa Clara Mission school were in the midst of a two-month term in mid December 1846. Olive vowed to educate the pioneer class to the best of her ability and protect them from any harm. The gun that swung from the belt of her gingham dress when it wasn't in her arms assured her students they were safe.

Olive was born on October 8, 1824, in Ashtabula, Ohio. She was one of a family of fifteen and a favorite of her uncle, Horace Mann, a leader in American education. His belief that a "common school education benefited both the individual and the community at large" had a profound effect on Olive. She entered the teaching field as a teenager and for several years worked in a variety of schools in the Ohio region.

Olive married Dr. Isaac Chauncey Isbell on March 4, 1844. Isaac was a medical graduate of the Western Reserve College in Wadsworth. Four months after the wedding, the newlyweds moved to Greenbush. Isaac established a thriving practice, and Olive concentrated on teach-

ing at the local school. Within two years the pair had saved more than
$2,000 from their respective jobs. During that time they encountered
numerous people interested in going west to help settle the wild frontier, but neither Isaac or Olive considered moving themselves until
they read a circular describing the splendors of California.

Isaac sought help to organize a trip overland from Jacob and
George Donner. The Donners made arrangements for Isaac and
Olive to join the Aram-Imus wagon train in Springfield, Illinois.
After purchasing a wagon, team, and supplies, the Isbells set out for
the Gold Country with a caravan of travelers. On April 14, 1846,
the Isbells' covered wagon fell in line with thirty-one other wagons
and crossed the Mississippi River near Fort Madison. Charles Imus
and Joseph Aram led the way. Olive had the utmost faith in Joseph.
He was a well-respected guide and credited with opening the route
across the Sierras by way of the Cold Stream and Emigrant Canyon
into the Sacramento Valley.

As for most pioneers making the long trip across the country, the
journey was arduous. Hauling themselves and their belongings over
the rough water of the Platte River was harrowing. They endured the
tortures of thirst in the Salt Lake Desert and encountered hostile
Indians that threatened to end their lives and take their livestock. The
weather at times was uncooperative, cholera overcame some of the
pioneers, and many animals were lost to exhaustion.

Although the hardships were overwhelming at times, Olive
enjoyed the camaraderie with the other sojourners and the wild game
that was in abundance along the trail. In the evenings the weary
men, women, and children would sit around the campfire feasting
on roasted turkey and venison stew and share their dreams of life in
a new land.

When the Aram-Imus wagon train reached Fort Laramie, Wyoming, they met a panic-stricken pioneer and his wife and children

charging through the post, warning everyone to turn around and head back in the direction they came. The people on the frontier beyond the fort were engaged in a war with Mexico.

"Anyone crossing the mountains will be exterminated," the frantic man announced.

"What shall we do," Olive recalled asking her husband. "I started for California and I want to go on," she recorded in her journal.

Her determination and spirit prompted others to continue the journey as well. The majority of the wagon trains pressed on, some heading to Oregon and others to the Gold Country.

"When the company separated to head off in different directions there wasn't a dry eye among us," Olive recalled years later. Traveling the rough trail together had made them friends and they departed doubting they would ever see one another again.

Joseph Aram escorted the wagon train the Isbells were with toward the Sierra Nevada Mountains. It took sixteen days to cross the range and settle on the other side. No wagons or lives were lost in the process. As there was no clear trail, the company had to make its own roads. Once they forded the Bear River, they made camp in a lush field near the water's edge. Olive and the wagon master's wife tackled the laundry that had piled up and made an interesting discovery when they laid the items out to dry.

"The clothes were heavy with particles of something that glittered in the sun," Olive noted in her journal. "What do you suppose it is?" asked Mrs. Aram. "I think it is isinglass I replied."

Two years later, when some of the richest deposits were found on Bear River, they decided that they might have had the privilege of being gold discoverers had they known gold when they saw it.

Olive, Isaac, and the other members of the company were led to Sutter's Fort by a member of Colonel John C. Fremont's battalion who had been patrolling the trail. The same officers accompanied the group to the Santa Clara Mission, 150 miles south of the fort, late in October 1846. The mission was under attack; and after unloading the women and children from the wagons and making sure they were safe, the able-bodied men with the group joined Fremont's men in the fighting. Dr. Isbell was among the recruits willing to do battle with General Sanchez and his growing army. His time in battle was interrupted when he succumbed to typhoid pneumonia and was forced to return to the mission.

In the midst of nursing her husband back to health and withstanding the exchange of daily gunfire between Fremont's and Sanchez's troops, Olive had to wage war against the elements. Heavy rains drenched the area and strong winds threatened to destroy the mission's structure. The wet and cold weather made the residents ill. Fever overtook them and many died. With Dr. Isbell's instruction, Olive helped arrest the sickness and prevented infection from settling in the lungs. She dealt out more than a hundred doses of medicine a day. When she wasn't tending to the sick she was getting ammunition to the soldiers.

Outnumbered and with supplies dwindling, they dispatched messengers to a military post in Yerba Buena asking for help in rescuing the mission. A number of Marines and Navy men answered the call and, as soon as they arrived, assisted the weary soldiers in fighting back the Mexican army. Olive tended to the wounded, dressing wounds and removing bullets.

It was while the sick were convalescing that Olive decided to gather all the children in the mission together and start the English-speaking school system.

"It was more my desire to relieve the ailing, sorely tired mothers that I did it," she later confessed, "more so than to accomplish much in the way of education, for the project was wholly a labor of love."

The Mexican army laid down its arms and agreed to stop fighting in late December 1846. A truce was declared on January 3, 1847.

Two months after the fighting stopped, Olive and her still frail husband, along with five other families, relocated to Monterey. When Dr. Isbell was well enough, he resumed his medical practice. He and Olive also purchased an inn. Called the Washington Hotel, the two-story adobe house was the first American hotel in the area.

Olive's reputation as a teacher and the work she did at the mission prompted local landowners to ask her to establish a school in Monterey. On the first day of school, twenty-five students assembled at a one-room class that was located upstairs from the town jail. Parents were charged $1 a month for their children to attend. Twenty-six additional pupils enrolled within the first month classes were in session. The large room was furnished with an adequate number of desks and benches. Several of the students owned their own readers and spellers and readily shared their materials with the children who did not. Pencils and paper were offered to everyone free of charge. More than half the class spoke Spanish only. Although Olive spoke no Spanish, she was able to do her job with the assistance of a couple of bilingual students.

The Monterey School was successful, as was the Washington Hotel, but Dr. Isbell was restless. In October 1847, he sold their property and ventured into the cattle business. The couple bought a ranch north of Stockton, California, and moved into a new, one-room log cabin in the center of the sprawling acreage.

Rumors of gold being found in the streams and riverbeds in the foothills convinced Isaac to leave his wife to find a rich strike. Olive recalled in her journal the event that sent her husband sprinting towards the gold fields:

The Wimmer family, who went to Sutter's Mill in 1848, had passed the winter with us at the mission in 46. The doctor ushered a new little Wimmer into the world, and altogether the families had kept in as close touch as possible with each other. Mrs. Wimmer was a native of Georgia, born near gold mines. Unlike most other Californians, she knew gold when she saw it. From the beginning of their residence at the mill, particles of something glittering in the water brought into the house had been the subject of much discussion among the workmen.

Each had his opinion as to what it might be, but Mrs. Wimmer from the first said it was gold, only to be laughed at by the men. Everyday when water was poured at the table, there was much joking at what they called "Mrs. Wimmer's gold," but despite the fun at her expense she insisted that the sparkles in the water were surely gold.

On the historic morning of January 24, 1848, Mrs. Wimmer was doing the family washing under a tree. Seeing Marshall walking slowly toward her, she called: "What is it, Marshall?" "I believe it is gold," he replied. "Bring it here," she said, "put it in my suds. If it comes out bright it is gold. If it turns black it is not gold." The nugget went into the suds and came out bright, as all the world knows.

Not only did Olive keep up with the work around the ranch during the time her husband was off searching for gold, but she furnished provisions and food to travelers passing through as well. Meals of beef stew, omelets, hot rolls, and coffee with sugar and cream were $1 each in gold dust. Chickens sold for $5 each, butter $2 per pound, and eggs were $3 a dozen. Olive earned additional money making short, calico gowns and petticoats. The garments were highly sought after by the emigrants and cost two ounces of gold each.

After three years prospecting, Dr. Isbell returned home carrying eighty pounds of gold with him. One kidney-shaped nugget he found weighed seven pounds three ounces. The valuable nugget was sold to an Englishman in San Francisco who sent it on to the Bank of England to be put on display.

In 1850, the Isbells sold the Stockton ranch and moved back to Ohio. Ever the vagabond, Dr. Isbell soon left the area with his wife and moved to Texas. Using the fortune they made in California, the couple purchased yet another ranch and for more than ten years raised hundreds of heads of cattle near the Panhandle. By mid 1865, the Isbells had returned to California. They settled in the Ojai Valley in Ventura County.

Dr. Isbell died in 1886 after a tragic horse-and-buggy accident. Olive lived out her last years in Santa Paula, tending to the livestock and counseling future teachers on the profession.

Historians recognize Olive Mann Isbell as the first American schoolteacher in California. Santa Paula city officials celebrated the contribution she made to the field of education by naming a school there in her honor.

Lucia Darling

THE MONTANA TEACHER

"They have had much to do in winning the west; and a higher civilization has always followed closely in the footsteps of the woman pioneer."

—LUCIA DARLING, 1875

The sprawling mining community of Bannack, Montana, was awash in the far-reaching rays of the morning sun. The rolling hills and fields around the crowded burg were thick with brush. Saffron and gold plants dotted the landscape, their vibrant colors electric against a backdrop of browns and greens. Twenty-seven-year-old Lucia Darling barely noticed the spectacular scenery as she paraded down the main thoroughfare of town. The hopeful schoolmarm was preoccupied with the idea of finding a suitable place to teach. Escorted by her uncle, Chief Justice Sidney Edgerton, Lucia made her way to a depressed section of the booming gold hamlet searching for the home of a man rumored to have a building to rent.

Referring to a set of directions drawn out on a slip of paper, Lucia marched confidently to the door of a rustic, rundown log cabin and knocked. When no one answered right away, Chief Justice Edgerton took a turn pounding on the door. Finally, a tired voice called out from the other side for the pair to "come in."

The interior of the home was just as unkempt as the outside. Cobwebs clung to the dark corners, dust inches thick covered dilapidated

Mrs. Lucia Darling Park, Warren, Ohio, June 1904

pieces of furniture, mining equipment, picks, pans, and axes were scattered about as well as a few dirty clothes, and an assortment of whisky bottles. A pile of buffalo robes in the middle of the floor stirred, and a scruffy prospector, obviously suffering with a monstrous hangover, emerged. Lucia and the chief justice introduced themselves and informed the man that they were there to look at some property he owned that could possibly be used as a schoolhouse. "Yes," the miner responded with a thick tongue. "Damn shame, children running around the streets here. They ought to be in school. I will do anything I can to help. You can have this room."

Lucia gave the man a polite smile and made her way around the room examining the space. Eager to come to an arrangement, the miner reiterated his belief that children needed to be educated and reaffirmed how willing he was to make that possible. The moment Chief Justice Edgerton asked about the price the man began tidying up a bit and cursing about the state of the space.

"Well, I'll do anything I can. I'll give it to her cheap," the miner assured Lucia and her uncle. "She shall have it for $50 a month. I won't ask a cent more. It's dirt cheap." The Chief Justice thanked the man for his time, and he and Lucia exited the crude dwelling. The persistent prospector stood in the doorway repeating his desire to be generous and help the children.

"Fifty dollars a month for a broken down structure that had mud plastered walls inside and out, a mud roof and dirt floors?" Lucia said to her uncle as she shook her head. "I believe his generosity extends only to himself," she added under her breath.

Lucia began her search for a suitable classroom in late September 1863. After turning down the greedy prospector's offer to use his building, she spent another month trying to locate a suitable facility. Due to the exorbitant cost to rent even the most modest space, Lucia decided to teach school from her uncle's sizeable and comfortable home.

"The school was opened in a room in our own house," Lucia remembered in her journal, "on the banks of the Grasshopper Creek near where the ford and foot bridge were located, and in hearing of the murmur of its waters as they swept down from this mountain country through unknown streams and lands in the distant sea."

Lucia Darling's desire to become an educator began when she was a young girl growing up in Tallmadge, Ohio. She was born in 1839 to dedicated farming parents who did not place as much emphasis on learning to read and write as they did the ability to complete chores. Lucia did, however, excel at reading, history, and math, and passed along what she knew to her brothers and sisters. When she was old enough, she received the proper training necessary to become a qualified teacher.

After more than nine years of service in the area of northeast Ohio and teaching at Berea College, the first interracial college in Kentucky, Lucia decided to travel west. Educators were woefully lacking in the western regions, and she hoped to build and grow a frontier school wherever she settled.

On June 1, 1863, Lucia gathered her belongings and left home with her uncle, Sidney Edgerton and his family and headed to Lewiston, Idaho. Edgerton was a politician, a representative from Ohio, who had been appointed U.S. judge for the territory of Idaho. The estimated three-month-long trip was being made so he could take over the position. Although Lucia would not have a group of children to teach while on the trail, she wanted the trek to be educational for her future pupils. Throughout the entire journey Lucia kept a detailed diary. The diary outlined the route they took, the Indians they encountered, the historic landmarks they passed, the daily chores that had to be done, and the weather patterns.

Lucia and her family started their travel via railroad from Tallmadge to Chicago, then on to Quincy and St. Joseph. From there they boarded a riverboat and floated along the Missouri River to Omaha. Lucia described Omaha as an "isolated frontier town, built largely of logs with few houses more than one story in height. The great territorial capital of the bluff looked down upon the little hamlet, keeping over it citizens, watch and ward."

The trip from Omaha west was made by covered wagon. As was customary, the party was joined by other wagon trains heading in the same direction. Lucia introduced herself to the members and hoped they would all become fast friends. The wagon train would venture more than 500 miles across the vast prairie to its final destination. One of Lucia's first journal entries describes how exhausting the trip would be to make:

June 16—Our camp life has commenced and I am lying here on my back in a covered wagon with a lantern standing on the mess box at the back end of it.

Have pinned back the curtain so as to let the light shine in but it is so situated that I have to hold my book much above my head to see. Will write 'till the light goes out. We left the Herndon tonight after tea our wagons having gone on some hours before. Most of the oxen are young—never having been driven before and they were determined to go every way but the right way. The drivers—Gridley, Chipman, Booth, and Harry Tilden were completely tired out trying to drive them. They scurried perfectly wild and ran from one side to another of the road, smashed through fences and finally broke one yoke in pieces.

Poor weather conditions posed numerous problems for the pioneers. Learning how to keep precious belongings safe from a light rain as well as keeping food dry during torrential downpours wasn't an easy task. According to notes Lucia made in her journal in mid-June 1863, a storm hit just as the sojourners were preparing to set up camp one evening:

> *June 17—Wednesday. We truly had quite a time yesterday and today has been a continuation of the same thing. . . . Went about three miles and camped on a small creek for the night. Uncle Edgerton and Gridley guarding the cattle. We had hardly time to get our things ready for the night when it commenced to blowing terribly—the thunder and lightening indicating a dreadful shower.*
>
> *Here I stand with my back against the front curtains of the wagon to keep it from blowing in and writing by the light of the lantern I have hung out to let those who are out guarding know where the camp is. The wind is blowing a perfect hurricane and every gust threatens to take off the wagon covers. The occupants of the tent find it more than they can do to keep it upright. The situation is quite alarming. The lighting at every flash seems to envelop us in a sheet of white flame and the rain pours in torrents.*

Everyone on the train had specific jobs for which they were responsible. Some cared for the livestock, others gathered wood and tended to the children. On June 21, 1863, Lucia took a moment to give an "account of everyday pioneering life" and outlined some of her own duties:

> *June 21—The first thing in the morning of course is breakfast and as Aunt Mary and Cousin Hattie are busy with the children that duty mostly falls upon me with Amarette's help. I usually find the*

fire built in the little stove standing at the back end of the wagons and as there is only one course at breakfast it does not take long to prepare it—coffee, ham, or bacon, biscuit or griddle cakes or both, gravy and plenty of milk. Before setting the table it has to be made each time by taking the boards from the front end of the wagon an placing one end under the back part of the corner of the mess box which is sloping, and letting it rest on the front side of the box make it nearly level. Three of these boards form quite a table on which we put a table cloth, tin plates and cups, knives, forks, spoons, etc. . . . The milk is strained into a large tin-can and hung under the wagon. Our wagons are so arranged that the things can be put back from the front during the day and chairs can be set in or we can sit or lie down on the bed at the back of the wagon. The wagon covers have been a good protection from the sun this far. We make a stop of an hour or two at noon and then try to get into camp in time to get supper and do up the work, get the cows milked and the tent pitched before dark.

On July 3 Lucia and the other party members crossed the Platte River, and it was on the other side of the river where they had their first encounter with Native Americans.

"Heard the startling news that only five miles below us there were fifteen hundred Sioux Indians," Lucia wrote. "They had come out to fight the Pawnees so we did not fear them much. We should be perfectly powerless if they had attacked us, but they did not, and in fact we see no signs of Indians nor have we but once since we left Omaha."

By July 16, 1863, the wagon train Lucia was a part of reached Chimney Rock, the most famous landmark on the Oregon, California, and Mormon Trails. Nearly half a million westbound emigrants and other travelers saw the monument en route to the West

Coast. Many of those emigrants drew sketches of Chimney Rock as they passed. Lucia was content to write about the stone formation in her journal:

July 16—Thursday. Near noon came in sight of the renowned Chimney Rock and the first sight of it was really like a chimney. The atmosphere was smoky and made the rock seem more like a large chimney from some great manufacturing establishment from which the smoke had settled down over the surrounding country. It seemed quite near us when we camped at noon and Hattie and I were determined to go over it but all said we were crazy, we could never get there . . . however we started with Henry and Wilbur with the pleasing assurance from Mr. Booth that it was seven miles at least.

In the midst of the hardship of frontier travel, Lucia and the other members of her party found ways to enjoy themselves. They collected wildflowers, swam in swift, cold riverbeds, and in the evenings around the campfire some pioneers played musical instruments while others sang and danced along.

On August 13, 1863, the wagon train stopped at a small military camp of twenty Ohio soldiers. A celebration of sorts was held that night to welcome the emigrants to the scene.

"We are in camp near their barracks and they seem very glad to see anyone from the States," Lucia penned in her journal. "A soldier's life here is very monotonous and very uncomfortable in winter. During the evening the soldiers came over and sat around the stove and Mr. Everett brought over his violin and we had a swing. After we had finished singing the soldiers danced a cotillion or two which they entered into with energy."

On a good day the wagon train could travel between fifteen to twenty miles. When the day's journey ended, people took turns guarding the vehicles and livestock in the evenings. On September 3, 1863, Lucia stood in as a lookout for her uncle.

"I sat up and watched the cattle and the stars all night with our Indian pony for company," she recalled in her diary. "The number of Indians and bears I saw on each side of the camp among the willows in the moonlight I did not count, but have decided today in broad daylight that it was all my imagination. Uncle set his gun out of the tent and I kept my revolver close to me. Wonder what I would have done if I had seen one, either a bear or Indian. I presume I should have screamed, perhaps not."

The driven schoolteacher arrived in Bannack, Montana, in mid-September 1863. An onslaught of winter weather kept the wagon train from moving on into Idaho. It was decided that the pioneers would stay there until the spring. The drive west had been a trying one for Lucia, but the sight of a civilized town after three and a half months on the trail made her temporarily forget the struggles.

"In looking back to that journey from Ohio," she recalled in her diary, "I think of nothing that interested us more than our arrival in Bannock. The growth of a day whose existence and fame went hand in hand and spread over the entire contingent in a single season."

Bannack was a wild and wooly gold-mining town. It was founded in 1862 by a prospector named John White who dipped his pan into nearby Grasshopper Creek and came up with chunks of glittering yellow rock. News of the rich gold deposits in the area spread quickly. Miners, businessmen, and families rushed to the spot. By 1863 more than three thousand residents lived there.

The remote location of the thriving town made it difficult for explorers to readily find. Signs posted along the trail into Bannack that read KEPE TO THE TRALE NEXT TO THE BLUFFE and TU GRASS HOPPER DIGGINGS 30 MYLES helped guide people to the destination.

Lucia's time in Montana was supposed to be brief, but her uncle decided they should stay on and help make Bannack the first territorial capital. Her time in the region turned out to be indefinite after the chief justice was named governor.

"Bannack was tumultuous and rough," Lucia wrote in her journal. "It was the headquarters of a band of highwaymen. Lawlessness and misrule seemed to be the prevailing spirit of the place."

She was referring to a group of desperados led by Sheriff Henry Plummer. Plummer and his deputies pretended to arrest robbers and thieves terrorizing the area, but were actually leading the bandits who perpetrated the crimes. He was eventually found out, captured, and hanged from his own gallows.

In the midst of the civil unrest were law-abiding homesteaders and parents who were anxious to have their children in school. Lucia was asked to take charge of locating a schoolhouse and acting as the town's first teacher. Equipping the classroom with the tools needed to start class was difficult. Makeshift chairs and desks had to be acquired as well as books on a variety of subjects.

When the first term began in mid 1864, children met at the Edgerton home for morning sessions. By the fall semester, students were meeting at a cabin that had been built specifically for use as a school.

"I cannot remember the name of all the scholars in that school," Lucia wrote in her journal in 1904. "I very much regret to say that, and I know where only a few of them are living, at the opening of the twentieth century. . . . A few pupils of mine are scattered in other lands. I trust that all of them are living, and remember affectionately our Bannack University of humble pretensions, but which sought to fulfill its mission and which, so far as I know, was the first school taught within what is now the state of Montana."

In 1868 Lucia left Montana to teach school in the southern states to children who had been denied the chance to learn. She was part of the Freeman's Bureau, an organization founded in 1865 to help black communities establish schools and churches. In addition to teaching, Lucia wrote stories about her experience as an educator and had several of those articles published in magazines.

No matter where the work took her, she recalled the time spent teaching in Montana as one of the most rewarding adventures she ever embarked on.

"Since that remote time (in Montana)," she recalled in her journal, "I have been identified for a period with one of the historic schools of the country of some repute, usefulness and promise; but I look back to the days I spent striving to help the little children in Bannack with a profound gratification. The school was not pretentious, but it was in response to the yearning for education, and it was the first."

Sarah Royce

The Philosopher's Teacher

"If we were going, let us go and meet what we were to meet bravely."

—Sarah Royce's comments about the trip
to California, April 30, 1849

The long shadows of a beleaguered wagon train stretched across the Carson River Route, a parched trail through Nevada. Pioneers traveling west used this unavoidable route to get to California. The long, dry crossing was one of the most dreaded ordeals of the entire emigrant experience. The sources of fresh, drinkable water were forty miles apart from one another. Thirty-year-old Sarah Royce had read about the desolate section of land in the fragments of a guide book she'd found while on the journey to the Gold Country in 1849. By the time many of the sojourners had reached this part of the trek their wagons and livestock weren't fit to continue.

Sarah, her husband, and their two-year-old daughter, Mary, stared in amazement at the abandoned vehicles and carcasses of ox and mule teams lying about. It seemed to the weary couple that they could walk over the remains of the animals for the duration of the trip and never touch the ground. The grim markers were nothing Sarah envisioned she would see when she embarked on the six-month venture. Having left her home in Iowa to follow the hordes of other pilgrims hoping to find gold, she set her sights on a serene and profitable life in a country depicted as a utopia. The expedition had proved to be more difficult than she had expected. As she recalled in her diary:

> *While making our way over the desert we came upon a scene of a wreck that surpassed anything preceding it. . . . As we neared it, we wondered at the size of the wagons which, in the dim light of the moon, looked tall as houses, against the sky. . . . We turned to look at what lay round the monster wagons. It would be impossible to describe the motley collection of things of various sorts, strewed all about . . . . There was only one thing, (besides the few pounds of bacon) that, in all these varied heaps of things, many of which, in civilized scenes, would have been valuable, I thought worth picking up. That was a little book, bound in cloth and illustrated with a number of small engravings. It's title was "Little Ella." I thought it would please Mary, so I put it in my pocket. It was an easily carried souvenir of the desert; and more than one pair of eyes learned to read its pages in after years.*

As a natural educator, Sarah was drawn to items that would teach children. Her parents encouraged that gift when she was very young and encouraged her to study a variety of subjects from religion to world cultures. She was born Sarah Eleanor Bayliss in Stratford upon Avon, England, in 1819. Her mother and father moved to America when she was six weeks old and settled in New York. She excelled in every area of school and was a voracious reader. She graduated from Phipps Union Female Seminary and became a schoolteacher in Rochester. After she met and married Josiah Royce Sr., the two relocated to the Midwest. Shortly after the birth of their first child, they traveled to Missouri and began preparing to head west.

Seated in a wagon filled with all her worldly possessions, Sarah, along with the other men, women, and children in their party, left

Independence on April 30, 1849. The first day of the journey was uneventful. They stopped to eat a "pleasant lunch on the prairie" and when the trip resumed she watched the afternoon "wear quietly away."

The mundane beginning would not be sustained.

The roads were rough, the weather either too cold or too hot, and unexpected problems, like the livestock wandering off, continually arose.

"It soon became plain that the hard facts of this pilgrimage would require patience, energy, and courage fully equal to what I had anticipated when I had tried to stretch my imagination to the utmost," Sarah wrote in her journal.

At various stops along the way, the Royces met with other emigrants making the move—families with the same visions of happily-ever-after that Sarah possessed. When they reached a post well along the Missouri River, news of the grasslands between Kansas and Colorado having been eaten up by the stock from other wagon trains and of an outbreak of cholera made Sarah reconsider going any further. Josiah managed to persuade her to continue on.

On June 11, 1849, Sarah and her family reached Council Bluffs, Iowa. A week after their arrival a ferryboat transported their wagons, belongings, and pack animals across the Missouri River. She wouldn't eat a meal or sleep a single night inside a house until she reached Fort Laramie, Wyoming. She wrote in her journal later that "outside of our wagons there were not homes or shelter anywhere along the vast wilderness we came."

Among the difficulties that presented themselves to Sarah and her fellow travelers were the Plains Indians. Frustrated by the invasion of white settlers of their ancestral lands, the tribes sought restitution against the hordes of interlopers. As Sarah recounted in her journal:

As we drew nearer, to what was initially thought to be buffalo, they proved to be Indians, by hundreds. And soon they had arranged themselves along each side of the way. A group of them came forward, and at the Captain's command our company halted, while he with several others went to meet the Indians and hold a parley. It turned out they had gathered to demand payment of a certain sum per head for every emigrant passing through this part of the country, which they claimed as their own. The men of our company after consultation, resolved that the demand was unreasonable! That the country we were traveling over belonged to the United States, and that the red men had no right to stop us. The Indians were then plainly informed that the company meant to proceed at once without paying a dollar. That if unmolested, they would not harm anything; but if the Indians attempted to stop them, they would open fire with all their rifles and revolvers. At the Captain's word of command all the men of the company then armed themselves with every weapon to be found in their wagons.

Revolvers, knives, hatchets, glittered in their belts; rifles and guns bristled on their shoulders . . . we were at once moving between long, but not very compact rows of half naked redskins. . . . After a while they evidently made up their minds to let us pass, and we soon lost sight of them.

Sarah and the other pioneers on the train formed close friendships. They helped each other through misgivings they had about the trip, shared food and supplies, nursed one another back to health, and gave proper burials to those who didn't recover. Whenever a sojourner was lost along the way, Sarah recalled the "heavy gloom that surrounds the emigrants."

"We couldn't help but wonder who would go next," she wrote. "What if my husband should be taken and leave us alone in the wilderness? What if I should be taken and leave my little Mary motherless? Or, still more distracting a thought—what if we both should be laid low, and she be left a destitute orphan, among strangers, in a land of savages? Such thoughts would rush into my mind, and for some hours these gloomy forebodings heavily oppressed me; but I poured out my heart to God in prayer, and He gave me comfort and rest."

At the end of each day the leader of the train would direct the company of wagons into a large circle. The cattle or oxen were unhitched and the tongue of each vehicle was laid at the end of the wagon in front. After the animals had a chance to graze and get water, they were led into the center of the circle for their protection and to keep them from running off. While the men tended to the livestock, Sarah and the other women were busy cooking, mending clothes, and caring for the children.

By July 4 Sarah's wagon train had made it to Chimney Rock in Nebraska. They stopped to celebrate Independence Day and to give thanks for making it as far as they had. Sarah used the sights and sounds experienced on the trek as lesson objects for her daughter. She climbed Independence Rock with her little girl, teaching her about landmarks and distances.

"Of course I had to lift her from one projection to another most of the way," Sarah later wrote. "But we went leisurely and her delight on reaching the top, our short rest there, and the view we enjoyed, fully paid for the labor."

After leaving Independence Rock, the teacher and her family pressed along the Mormon Trail to the Great Salt Lake Basin. On August 30, 1849, Sarah and her husband decided to set off on their own and cross the Salt Desert. The majority of the party they had traveled with wanted to use a new, virtually untried route into California.

The Royces did not trust the so-called "experimental guide" who had plans to start the venture in October. At a date so late in the year, Josiah believed the way would be impassable by snow. The Royces and a few other families took the usual trail to their destination.

"Our only guide from Salt Lake City consisted of two small sheets of note paper, sewed together and bearing on the outside in writing the title 'Best Guide to the Gold Mines, 816 Miles, by Ira J. Wiles, GSL City.'"

Sarah and her family encountered more Indians on their journey. They would hide along the trail and ambush travelers as they passed. Josiah maintained a strong, businesslike stance against the Natives, refusing to give up any livestock or provisions. His resistance rattled the Indians, and they eventually let the Royces' wagon train continue on.

The Salt Lake Desert and the Carson River Route were the most grueling parts of the journey for Sarah. Violent thunder- and windstorms halted travel and threatened to leave them stranded forever in the desolate locations. The intense heat of the sun forced them to make their way by night. They were thirsty, exhausted, and disoriented much of the time.

Sarah remembered:

It was moonlight, but the gray-white sand, with only here and there sagebrush, looked all so much alike that it required care to keep to the road. And now, for the first time in my life, I saw a mirage; or several repetitions of that optical illusion. Once it was an extended sheet of water lying calmly bright in the moonlight with here and there a tree on its shores; and our road seemed to tend directly towards it; then it was a small lake seen through openings in a row of trees, while the shadowy outlines of a forest appeared beyond it; all lying to

our left. What a pity it seemed to be passing it by, when our poor ani-
mals had been so stinted of late. Again, we were traveling parallel
with a placid river on our right; beyond which were trees; and from
us to the water's edge the ground sloped so gently it appeared absurd
not to turn aside to its brink and refresh ourselves and our oxen.

Sarah, Josiah, and their daughter arrived on the other side of the desert on October 17, 1849, and faced the towering Sierra Nevada Mountains. Stormy weather had already deposited a heavy layer of snow over the rocky range. Following after her husband and their pack mules as they made their ascent, Sarah held her child closely with one arm and held tightly to the branches and bushes along the mountain wall with the other. At night they had no choice but to make camp near snow-covered bluffs. Their water supply turned to ice and campfires had to be constantly maintained to keep them from dying out and the wagon train from freezing to death.

On October 19, 1849, Sarah celebrated the progress they'd made climbing the mountains. She was closer to her new home and wrote in her journal that "hope now sprang exultant."

"We were to cross the highest ridge, view the promised land and begin our descent into warmth and safety," she recalled. "So, without flinching I faced steps still steeper than the day before: I even laughed in my little one's upturned face, as she lay back against my arm, while I leaned forward almost to the neck of the mule, tugging up the hardest places."

The Royces reached the growing gold-mining town of Weaverville in late October, pitched their tent, and "began to gather about [them] little comforts and conveniences, which made [them] feel as though [they] once more had a home," Sarah remembered.

With the exception of her Bible, a book by Milton, and a tiny lap desk, Sarah had lost all her possessions en route to the Gold Country.

While Josiah searched for gold, Sarah maintained their canvas home. Lonely miners on their way to and from their claims often stopped to watch Sarah and Mary. It had been such a long time since they'd seen a woman or toddler they couldn't help themselves from staring. The men bowed courteously to Sarah and made mention of how Mary reminded them of their children they left behind in the East.

Josiah eventually abandoned mining and went into business with a pair of investors seeking to open a mercantile in town. Sarah and Mary accompanied him to Sacramento to purchase supplies. When they returned, a crude store had been constructed. The Royces lived in the back half of the building and managed the buying and selling of goods in the front half. During the course of the workday, Sarah would overhear prospectors lamenting over their decisions to come to California with the Gold Rush. Finding riches was not as easy as they dreamed it would be.

"They had to toil for days before finding gold," Sarah wrote in her journal, "and when they found it, had to work hard in order to wash out their 'ounce a day,' and then discovered that the necessaries of life were so scarce it took much of their proceeds to pay their way, they murmured; and some of them cursed the country, calling it a 'God forsaken land,' while a larger number bitterly condemned their own folly in having left comfortable homes and moderate business chances, for so many hardships and uncertainties."

After Sarah and her family suffered through an attack of the cholera-morbus (acute gastroenteritis), Sarah, her husband, and child moved to Sacramento to avoid other more serious illnesses that were circulating around Weaverville. From January 1850 to

1854, the Royces lived in a variety of thriving northern California towns. Among them were Folsum, San Francisco, and Martinez. In the spring of 1854, Sarah, Josiah, and their growing family of three, moved to Grass Valley, a popular mining location in the high Sierra Nevadas. They moved into a small house along the main thoroughfare that led to a ravine where prospectors were hunting gold. Shortly after their arrival Sarah gave birth to the couple's fourth child, Josiah Royce Jr.

Sarah devoted a great deal of time to educating her children. She taught them how to read using the Bible as a textbook. Astronomical charts, histories, and an encyclopedia of common and scientific knowledge were used as well to train the youngsters. Periodically, the children of other camp followers were sent to study with Sarah. The need was so great for a teacher in Grass Valley that she decided to open a school for young ladies and misses. Despite the fact that the main objective was to reach girls, it was co-educational, and the boys she taught included her own son, who went on to become a distinguished professor of philosophy at Harvard University.

Josiah Jr. fondly recalled his mother's classroom influence in his own memoirs published in the early 1900s:

My earliest teacher in philosophy was my mother, whose private school, held for some years in our own house, I attended, and my sisters, who were all older than myself, and one of whom taught me to read. I very greatly enjoyed my mother's reading of the Bible stories.

In 1857, Josiah Sr. went into business with a church friend and purchased several acres of farmland outside of Grass Valley. He named the large spread Avon Farm after Sarah's birthplace. Sarah continued to teach school while her husband raised a variety of crops and supplied the community with apples, peaches, and dairy products. More than nine years after they had moved to the mining town, the Royces returned to San Francisco.

Sarah's son called his mother an "effective teacher" and her journal, entitled the *Pilgrimage Diary* (which was published later in a volume entitled *A Frontier Lady)*, has been used for centuries to educate students. Studying her memoirs educates readers about the sights, terrain, and hardships of traveling over the plains.

Mary Gray McLench

The Oregon Teacher

"It seemed a wild, new place, with only a small sprinkling of houses scattered among trees and huge stumps."

—MARY GRAY McLENCH'S MEMORY OF A FRONTIER TOWN
IN OREGON SHE PASSED THROUGH ON HER WAY
TO HER FIRST TEACHING ASSIGNMENT
IN THE WEST, MARCH 1, 1901

On March 22, 1851, the steamship the *Empire City* arrived at the Isthmus of Panama. The sun was hanging low behind a bank of clouds, and the busy seaport lay in purplish twilight. Five ambitious schoolteachers stood on the deck of the vessel watching the crewmen weigh anchor. Elizabeth Miller, Sarah Smith, Elizabeth Lincoln, Margaret Woods, and Mary Gray were wide-eyed by the feverish activity. A crowd of hundreds blackened the pier in the middle distance. The curious bystanders were like ants on a jelly sandwich. Cannons, firing from the ship's bows to alert the harbor master that the *Empire City* was safely moored, rattled Mary, but a word from a deck-mate assuring her that it was routine procedure helped calm her down.

Like the other educators on board, Mary had never encountered anything quite as grand and foreign. Having been born and raised in the Green Mountains of southern Vermont, her experiences were

Mary Gray McLench

limited to the family farm and a nearby town. At the age of twenty-five, she consented to the journey to the Wild West to develop schools and teach in remote areas of the frontier. Mary Almira Gray had already been teaching students to read and write at a one-room schoolhouse in the village of Grafton, not far from her home. As the oldest of four children, she naturally took to helping her siblings learn, and when she was old enough, she decided to parlay her talent into a profession.

In the winter of 1850, Vermont governor William Slade recruited young women from all over New England to travel to the Oregon Territory to establish schools. Slade was also an agent with the National Board of Popular Education. The association was created to train and sponsor teachers and encourage them to go west. After learning that her aunt and uncle were going to be moving to Oregon, Mary agreed to go. They made the trip via wagon train, but Mary chose to sail. Traveling over the ocean was considered by many to be less hazardous than overland trips were, but it was still difficult. During the five-thousand-mile excursion, passengers faced exposure to deadly tropical diseases such as dysentery, yellow fever, and cholera. Scurvy, storms, starvation and lack of water took a toll as well.

Samuel R. Thurston, a delegate to congress from the Oregon Territory, accompanied Mary and the four other teachers on their journey. The National Board of Popular Education supplied the ladies with the $350 they needed to pay for their fare. The cost included the price of a ticket to cross the isthmus and a new saddle for use after they reached the coast. With the exception of a mild storm off the coast of Cape Hatteras and strong winds entering the Caribbean Sea, the trip was relatively uneventful with regards to the weather.

Once the women arrived at the isthmus and disembarked, they traveled by mule over the mountains to Panama where they boarded another ship to take them on to San Francisco. Congressman Thurston contracted a fever somewhere along the way and in spite of multiple doses of quinine, did not improve.

"Mr. Thurston seemed to grow worse speedily and lost much of his accustomed cheerfulness," Mary recalled years later.

We little thought, however, how dark a cloud was so soon to overshadow us. On Thursday night Mr. Thurston went to his stateroom sick, and some young men in his care watched over him. Sunday morning he was assisted to the captain's stateroom on deck, which the latter had kindly offered for the sick man's use, it being commodious and airy.

The disease (Isthmus of Panama fever, I suppose) was making rapid progress. Most of the time Mr. Thurston was conscious except during the last few hours. His death occurred early, not later than one o'clock, Wednesday morning, April 9th. Had he not been a public man, burial would have taken place at sea; but as it was, enshrouded or covered with the Stars and Stripes, our Country's flag, he was taken along on our course till Thursday morning, about nine o'clock, when our ship anchored near Acapulco. A coffin had been prepared on shipboard and he was laid to rest in the cemetery of that place.

Two politicians, Judge Thomas Nelson and Surveyor-General John B. Preston, consented to chaperone the women to their final destination. Neither was familiar with Oregon, but both were eager to lend their assistance. After more than a month at sea, the teachers landed in San Francisco on April 23, 1851. Mary found the city to be "considerably busy and expensive." She and the others stayed overnight at a posh hotel in town before heading out the next morning. She commented in her reminiscences about the cost and conditions of the accommodations:

The table (in the room) extending the length of the dining room, perhaps thirty feet, was good, and the viands delicious. Perhaps it was in honor of some sort of dress occasion.

I only remember Mrs. Gwin, who sat opposite me at supper, appeared costumed in black silk, with a large white lace cape and light kid gloves, ribbons, jewelry, etc.. At night the teachers and Miss Hyde occupied one large, unfinished room, on the door of which was posted a printed notice of prices. I only remember that board was $5.00 per day; lodging, $3.00 per night.

On April 24, 1851, a steamer carried the teachers up the Columbia River to Portland, Oregon. The population there was sparse—only fourteen thousand people resided in a territory that not only included Oregon, but Washington and Idaho as well. Six days later Mary and her fellow teachers boarded a flatboat covered with an awning and started for Oregon City. En route, the vessel ran into trouble. As Mary wrote:

"The best laid plans of mice and men aft gang aglee." When at the foot of Clackamas rapids, the boat ran aground. After a few ineffectual attempts to get it afloat, the craft was made fast to a tree on the shore. It was now getting dusk. The crew kindled a fire and began preparations for their supper, while the passengers were in the dark and supperless, notwithstanding that they could see lights into the houses at Oregon City.

General Preston unrolled two mattresses he had purchased in San Francisco, and arranged them for the ladies of the company so that they might get all the rest they could.

Early in the morning, baskets of provisions were sent down, and thus refreshed, we walked through a stumpy bushy pasture to Oregon City, which seemed to be much pleasanter and much more

of a place than Portland. Reverend Mr. Atkinson, to whose care the
teachers were assigned, met us and took us to his home.

In Oregon City, a town of fewer than seven hundred people, the
women received their individual assignments and were dispatched
to various locals. Sarah Smith remained in Oregon City; Elizabeth
Miller went west to Forest Grove; Elizabeth Lincoln and Sarah
Smith remained in Oregon City. Margaret Wands went to Durham.
Mary Gray began her school in Tualatin, a town 13 miles south of
Portland. Prior to making the long trip over the plains, Mary had
planned to return to live out her life close to her parents in Townsh-
end, Vermont. Her strong desire to go back to the East Coast ended
when she met Benjamin McLench. After she spent five terms teaching, the two married in the fall of 1852 and decided to stay in Oregon
and become farmers. The couple acquired 160 acres of land in the
Willamette River Valley through the Oregon Land Donation Act
and built a cabin on the spot.

Seven years and four children later, Mary and Benjamin were
successfully raising their family and growing several acres of wheat,
apples, onions, and potatoes. They also raised bees to make honey and
honey butter.

"The highest price received for wheat sold from our farm was
$4 a bushel, onions for $3, and potatoes for $4," Mary remembered.
"Our best price for butter was $.50 a pound. Bee swarms went for
$150 in a good year to $40 in other times."

Mary Gray McLench's memoirs were published in the spring
of 1900, fifty years after she came west to teach. In addition to
the recollections of her life with her husband and children, Frank,
Lizzie, and Alice (their fourth child died of pneumonia), Mary
included information about the other women who made the journey to Oregon with her:

In later years they all married and settled down in Oregon. Miss Smith became the wife of Alanson Beers, and stepmother to six children. After his death she married a Mr. Kline of Albany, I think, and the number of her step children increased in equal ratio. She became a widow the second time and died at the home of one of her daughters about twenty-five years ago.

Miss Woods became the second wife of Governor John P. Gaines, whose large family of children by the first wife returned to their Kentucky home, with the exception of two grown sons, who remained in Oregon. Governor Gaines died within a few years, and not many years afterwards Mrs. Gaines with one little daughter, returned to her friends in New York. Since then I know nothing in regard to her.

Miss Lincoln married Judge Alonza A. Skinner. He died many years ago, and she lived to an advanced age in Eugene, and died five or six years since.

Miss Miller married Joseph G. Wilson, and accompanied him to Washington after he was elected a member of Congress from Oregon. Before taking his seat they visited his old college town, Marietta, Ohio, where he became seriously ill and died suddenly. Mrs. Wilson returned to The Dalles and is still living there. She has three married daughters and one son, and lost three or four children in infancy. She was Postmistress at The Dalles for a number of years.

Sister Mary Russell and the Sisters of Mercy

THE ORPHANS' TEACHER

"Five Sisters of Mercy Arrived in Grass Valley from San Francisco."

—*HEADLINE ON THE FRONT PAGE OF*
THE GRASS VALLEY NEWSPAPER
THE UNION, *AUGUST 20, 1863*

Sister Mary Baptist Russell and four other nuns from the Sisters of Mercy Convent weaved their way around a parade of scruffy miners, traveling salesmen, and saloon girls crowded on a sturdy dock that was hugging a shore in San Francisco. Wearing black habits complete with scapulars, veils, and coifs, the women stepped aboard the steamer that was splattered with mud and dirt. The deck of the vessel was aswarm with prospectors en route to their diggings down river. Some were sleeping, others were playing cards or discussing their mining claims. The sisters inched their way to a clear spot near the bow and grabbed hold of the railing as the small craft moved slowly away from the landing.

The scene around the bay in August 1863 was chaotic. News of the discovery of gold north of the city had prompted people of every kind and description to pour into the place to gather supplies

Sister Mary Baptist Russell

before rushing to the hills. Men, women, and children were living in shacks, or sleeping on the ground under blankets draped over poles. The noise and pandemonium lessened considerably as the boat continued on past abandoned ships, old square-riggers, and new vessels anchored and waiting patiently for more eager passengers to come aboard.

The nuns smiled pleasantly at their fellow travelers before turning their attention to the golden brown landscape on either side of the clay-colored water. The furious mining activities in the mountains had left the once-clear river muddy and rolling; and fast-receding flood waters had left the once-deep channel shallow and treacherous. When Sister Russell spotted in the near distance a steamer that was stuck in the bars, she lifted her head to heaven in a silent prayer that their vessel would not suffer the same fate.

If the vessel did not get lodged in the mud and if a boiler did not explode, the trip between San Francisco and Sacramento was six hours. The intense heat and savage mosquitoes and fleas the nuns were forced to fight off made the trip seem longer. Sister Russell referred to the riverboat as that "miserable steamer"; and had it not been for the fact that the women were dedicated to care and educate children in the isolated mining camps, none would have ever chosen to leave the comforts of their San Francisco-based order.

The nuns who dared to make the journey had proven to the leaders of the church that they were most qualified for the job. They were strong, resourceful women who had provided food to hungry pioneers who had lost everything coming west, tended to cholera patients, and taught school to orphans.

Sister Russell had endured a number of hardships on her way from Ireland to California and was the leader of the group of traveling sisters. Born in County Down, Ireland, in 1829, she was only twenty-five years old when she came to America to help develop the rugged West. Like all the Sisters of Mercy she devoted her life to the service of the poor, the sick, and the ignorant. As a member of the Sisters of Mercy order in San Francisco, she helped establish St. Mary's Hospital, the oldest Catholic hospital in existence in California.

After a full day and night in the steamer, the nuns arrived in Sacramento. On August 20, 1863, they boarded a stage to take them onto their final destination, a mining camp called Grass Valley. The bells of St. Patrick's Church heralded their arrival and Father Thomas J. Dalton, the pastor who requested that the sisters come to the area, welcomed them with open arms and a blessing. He graciously gave up his home to the women, and for more than three years, the location served as their convent.

After moving their things into the makeshift convent, the women were escorted to the church and a small school that had already been built. Miss Johanna Fitzgerald was the sole educator of the 120 students that were enrolled, and her salary was $30 a month. As more wagon trains arrived in the area, the number of new pupils increased and more teachers were required. Sister Russell and the other nuns were to oversee the daily operations of the church parish and school as well as assist with the additional teaching duties. In exchange for their services, the Sisters of Mercy were promised $50 a month along with the fruits and vegetables from Father Dalton's garden.

Mount St. Mary's Academy, as it came to be known, was modeled on the Irish school system. There were three distinct levels of education: primary, secondary, and tertiary. The school was open to all children between the ages of six and fifteen. The majority of the pupils who were attending the school at the academy in 1863 were girls, and more than half of the student body was orphans. Mining accidents, disease, illness, starvation, hostile Indians, and inclement weather led to the demise of thousands of family members. Their ultimate deaths left countless children without a mother or father or both.

Struggling widows who had to provide for their helpless families looked to the church to keep a watchful eye on their youngsters while they worked.

Courtesy of the Grass Valley Museum

A classroom in the Mount St. Mary's school, Grass Valley, California

The sisters quickly recognized a need for an orphanage and a larger school and made plans to build such a facility a top priority. They managed to handle the overcrowded classrooms and lack of permanent housing for needy children for two years before the cornerstone of a new structure was laid. According to Sister Russell, the plans for the combination convent, school, and orphanage consisted of three working stories with the lower floor being designated for the kitchen, dining room, storerooms, laundry, lavatory, and primary school rooms. On the middle floor were more classrooms, the library, parlors, and a chapel for the sisters at the south end. On the third floor were the children's dormitories, the sisters' sleeping quarters, and the infirmary. The building was to measure 100 feet by 40 feet.

The doors of the new school and orphanage opened on March 20, 1866. The cost of the construction was of major concern to the nuns who felt entirely responsible for the more than $19,000 debt that had been incurred. They were adamant that the funds needed to pay the bills would not come from the indigent who attended or lived at the academy.

The school's 1865 directory notes, "There will be no charge for tuition under any circumstance in the Orphan Asylum, but where parents or guardians can afford it, the children boarding at the Orphanage will be charged for board at a rate of not exceeding $15 a month."

Believing that God would supply them the necessary capital to continue on with their endeavors, the sisters took in their first orphans on April 2, 1866. Another group of children arrived a few days later. The orphanage records indicate that they were "four most miserable creatures, blind and lame and poverty stricken in the extreme."

A mere eight months after the school and orphanage had started, there were sixty-nine children—fourteen boys and fifty-five girls—

under the nun's care. Through the help and support of a few bene-
factors, the Sisters of Mercy were able to furnish the facilities with
desks, beds, blankets, bedspreads, a kitchen store, and $150 worth of
utensils.

An unexpected, tragic event occurred before the school year
ended in 1866. A seven-year-old girl whose parents had wanted her
to have a Catholic education and had boarded her at the academy had
contracted pneumonia and died. The child's mother and father, her
classmates, and the sisters were overcome with grief, and there were
talks of postponing the completion of the term. After a great deal of
prayer, the nuns decided to continue on, and the first commencement
exercises were held in July 1867. More than three hundred people
attended the ceremony.

At the conclusion of the commencement program, Sister Russell turned her daily duties over to another capable sister and then
returned to the convent in San Francisco. She had served her post
well, but the order needed her considerable managerial skills at
home. It was with a heavy heart that she left the academy she so
loved.

As Mount St. Mary's grew in size so did its financial burdens.
Small amounts were donated to sustain the school and orphanage,
but creditors pressured the sisters to pay their bills in full. Although
they knew Sister Russell would have objected, the nuns reluctantly
decided the only way to get out of debt was to open a "select school
for young ladies" and charge them a fee to attend. For several
months local residents who had to send their daughters far away
for training at select academies had been petitioning the church to
start such a school. An advertisement announcing the sisters' intention to open a new institution appeared in the local newspaper in
September 1868.

Educational: To parents and guardians. The Sisters of Mercy, Grass Valley, realizing very sensibly the great pecuniary embarrassment under which the Institution under their control now labors, and anxious to contribute in every way possible to its success, have determined to open a select Day School for Young Ladies, which will be select in every particular and in which will be taught in addition to the English branches, the French and German languages, and vocal instrumental music. They are also prepared to accommodate a number of Boarding Scholars upon terms quite reasonable. They will endeavor to render complete satisfaction to persons entrusting to them the education of their children, and at reasonable rates of compensation.

The school would eventually be a profitable venture, but the bill collectors would not wait. The public rallied around the sisters hosting various fundraisers that netted enough to pay off most of their responsibilities. On the second anniversary of the Day School, the remaining debt was settled entirely.

By 1872 the Sisters of Mercy were maintaining three institutions: the school for boys and girls, the orphanage, and the boarding school for select young ladies. The staff of twenty nuns nurtured and educated more than two hundred students. Space to adequately teach the large number of incoming pupils dwindled, so that by 1875 a wing had to be added to the existing structure. Railroad service into the Grass Valley area a year later brought even more children to the school and forced the sisters to transform dormitories into temporary classrooms. Further additions were made to the academy in 1877 and 1878.

Regular school terms were occasionally interrupted to deal with outbreaks of scarlet fever, diphtheria, and smallpox. Children who were infected by the disease were isolated from the other students.

Some of the nuns would go into quarantine with the pupils to help care for them until the illness passed. During the long hours of separation, the sisters mended clothes, made quilts, read to one another, and reviewed lesson plans.

It cost fifty-five and a half cents a day to educate, feed, and clothe each child who lived at Mt. St. Mary's Academy. In 1879 there were 138 boarders and the cost per year was $26,415. The sisters received $9,000 a year in state aid and had to make up the difference of $17,415 on their own either from donations or benefactors. An advertisement placed in the *Grass Valley Union* newspaper in hopes of attracting students whose parents were willing to pay for a quality education ran in the summer of 1880. It listed the various costs of the programs and services available at the academy:

Board & Tuition per year	$150.00
Entrance Fee	$10.00
Washing per month	$2.00
Music per month	$6.00
Languages per year	$10.00
Fancy Work	$10.00
Painting & Drawing per month	$4.00

Enrollment did increase and annual budgets were satisfied. Pupils excelled in their course work and received high marks in their final examination. The exceptional standard of learning at the school was recognized in several articles of *The Union* newspaper. An item in the June 1886 edition praised the students who received top marks in their class and listed their various classes and their rankings. Here's an excerpt:

Mt. St. Mary's Convent
Standing in Final Examinations of the Graduating Class of 1886
June 12–17, 1886

Names	Gram.	Arith.	Lit.	Average	Standing
R. Dreyfus	96	96	93	93.25	V
L. Glidden	90	90	92	92	VI
M. Hall	94	88	94	93.37	III
M. Kelly	100	94	95	95.12	I
E. Murphy	92	97	94	93.50	II
E. Ryan	93	88	94	93.37	IV
G. Short	91	90	84	88	VII

An article two years later applauded the accomplishments of the teachers at Mount St. Mary's Academy and described the school's twentieth graduation ceremony, which took place in mid June 1888.

The commencement exercises at Mount St. Mary's Academy drew a very large and representative audience. In fact the music hall with its tiers and tiers of seats was inadequate to accommodate the throngs and a number of the ladies and gentlemen in attendance were obliged to content themselves with standing room. The worthy Sisters of Mercy were untiring in their exertions in behalf of their guests, and their thoughtful attentions and courtesies more than counterbalanced whatever inconveniences may have existed by reason of the overwhelming assemblage.

Flora emblems of the Catholic faith, lace curtains, well-considered illumination and other embellishments graced the hall and contributed to a harmonious effect which incited universal comment. Above and fronting the semi-circular array of pupils, and over filmy curtains, was suspended the motto, SUCCESS LEADS ON TO GREATER ENDEAVORS, done in gold tinsels.

Delightful symphony and, of course, perfect time, marked the instrumental numbers—a statement containing far more truth than compliment. When it is considered that as many as ten or twelve young ladies at times engaged in the execution of one selection, the force of these remarks will be more fully appreciated. The vocal music was good, while the essays were more than good. In these the choicest rhetoric was notable, and not a few new thoughts were forcible advanced. As rendered, the program was one of the best ever given in this city, and the instructors at the Academy indeed have reason for self-congratulation. The flattering remarks expressed by cultured ladies and gentlemen of last night's audience were well justified.

In response to a pressing invitation, Mr. M. B. Potter, the well-known educator, addressed the graduates and pupils generally, highly complimenting them for their efficiency, as displayed. He reviewed in brief, the Academy's rise and progress, enlivened the address with witty references. Rev. Frank Dalton spoke for a few minutes in very happy vein, and he with Father McDonnell conferred the honors upon the graduates and distributed the various premiums among the pupils.

In late September 1888, Sister Russell returned to the successful institution she helped found. She was suffering with a reoccurring throat condition, but her physicians agreed that a trip to Nevada County would be helpful for her condition. The Sisters of Mercy escorted the loyal nun around the grounds and showed her the changes that had been made to the school since she had left. She enjoyed walking under the thick pine trees and watching the orphans happily playing games.

After evaluating a couple of classes, Sister Russell was then taken to the nearby Idaho and North Star mines and watched the miners extract gold from the bowels of the earth.

She learned about high-grading during her visit and was amazed that the miners were required to change all their clothes at the end of each shift because some unscrupulous men hid gold in their garments. The time spent with the sisters and the pupils at the academy restored Sister Russell's health. When she went back to San Francisco, she was felling well and was able to serve another ten years at the convent.

Sister Russell died on August 6, 1898. San Francisco's St. Mary's Hospital, Grass Valley's Mount St. Mary's and many other Mercy foundations throughout the state of California, stand as a memorial to the work she did, and generations of students remembered the years she taught them to read and write.

Hannah Clapp

The University Teacher

"The present school is a credit both to the teachers and the town. It now numbers forty pupils, I should think, and is well and systematically conducted."

—REPORTER MARK TWAIN'S COMMENTS ABOUT THE
CARSON CITY SCHOOL HANNAH CLAPP
FOUNDED, JANUARY 14, 1864

On a bright, sunshiny day in mid July 1859, a dusty, travel-worn, weary schoolteacher named Hannah Clapp trudged into Salt Lake City, Utah. Dressed in a calico blouse and bloomers made of thick, canvas-type material and carrying a pistol, the thirty-five-year-old woman drew stares from the settlers, prospectors, and trappers milling about the main thoroughfare. Hannah made the trip west from Michigan with her brother, Nathan, his family, and a handful of other pioneers. The trip across the rough continent had been fraught with peril. The small wagon train had endured disease, starvation, inclement weather, and towering mountains, and had more of the same to look forward to before they would reach California.

Many emigrants were coaxed west by their desire for gold. Hannah was driven by a desire to bring formal education to frontier towns. An unattached female making the journey over the plains was as unconventional as Hannah's manner of dress. She was not affected by the attention her nonconformist behavior attracted. She was armed

Hannah Clapp

and ready to take on anyone who might physically challenge her style or dream of going to California to teach.

Hannah Keziah Clapp was born in Michigan in 1824. Little is known of her childhood or circumstances leading up to her pursuits as a teacher. The first mention of Hannah's work appeared in a Ypsilanti, Michigan, newspaper in 1847. It noted that her first job teaching was at a private school there. She entered the public school system a year later. In 1849 she moved to Lansing and taught at the Michigan Female Seminary College. Hannah was named the school's principal in 1854. During her time at the seminary she became active in women's issues and lobbied for women's rights. She all but abandoned the traditional clothing of women and much of the time wore "bloomer dresses"—trouserlike garments that reached to the ankle and were frilled at the cuff.

The wagon train Hannah traveled to Utah with stayed on in Salt Lake City for more than a week. The sojourners restocked their provisions and rested for a bit before continuing on with the trip. Hannah penned letters to friends back home describing the area and the people she met during the stopover. The letters were later published in the September 6, 1859 edition of the Lansing, Michigan, newspaper *The Republican*:

> *This Sunday is very much like other days with us here although now we have the privilege of attending a Mormon meeting. I embraced the opportunity on Sunday—went with my bloomer dress and hat, and with my revolver by my side. . . .*
>
> *Salt Lake is a large place, situated at the head of the great valley; on the east, the river Jordan; and on the east and north, laterally, mountains. Its first appearance, at a distance, looked like an Irish huddle; but on approaching it, it looked better. It is laid out in*

squares of forty rods each, streets crossing each other at right angles; and on either sides, streams of water, brought from the mountains for the purpose of irrigation, as it seldom rains here.

The buildings are made of adobe, a kind of sunburned brick; all unpainted except Brigham's Harem, this is painted a kind of cream. His buildings and garden occupy one square, and are enclosed with a stone wall twelve feet high, laid in lime mortar. Every rod are pillars built up four feet higher than the wall.

These are the "watchmen of the towers of Zion." Over the main door of this Harem is a huge lion, carved in marble, perhaps of the "tribe of Judah." On the top of the cupola is a bee-hive. Over the main gate is an eagle, with her wings spread. . . .

The man of the house where we put up while we were in the city, "The Utah House," had three wives. The first wife was very talkative. He was one and seventy, and kept preaching to me. One day he told me that "it would be the business of the Saints, in another world, to teach those of the gentiles that had not heard the gospel in this life; but he had preached to me, and he feared if I did not embrace the doctrine I would go to hell." I think Governor Cummings would consider my life in danger if he knew what I said to them. I will preach a little to the women when I get a chance, in spite of the Governor.

After arriving in California in late 1859, Hannah settled in a town 30 miles southwest of Sutter's Fort called Vacaville. She taught school there for less than a year and then decided to trek over the Sierras to bring education to the new territory of Nevada and take advantage of land grants promised to newcomers to the region.

Hannah arrived in Carson City in September 1860. Named after frontiersman and scout Kit Carson, the gold and silver boomtown was the hub of activity for miners and pioneers. A number of thriving businesses lined the main street and freight and transportation companies hustled a variety of goods from horses and cattle to coal and lumber to various points east. After learning there were no schools between the Sierras and Salt Lake City, Hannah went to work establishing a school in the area.

She began by petitioning the territorial leaders to approve a modest facility. Then in 1861 she helped get a bill passed to create a chartered school and the sum of $12,000 was appropriated to aid in the enterprise. In the spring of that year the doors of the Sierra Seminary were opened for coed enrollment. Miss Eliza C. Babcock and a Mrs. Cutler shared the teaching duties with Hannah. The three taught students ranged in age from kindergarten to high school. After graduation many of Hannah's pupils went on to great prominence. Among the accomplished scholars was inventor George Ferris, the man who designed the Ferris Wheel.

Hannah's students described her as a "brisk, outspoken woman with a round face, pink cheeks, bright blue eyes, and short curly hair."

"She always wore dark suits and good, sensible flat heeled shoes," former pupil Helen Fulton Peterson noted in her memoirs. "I never tired of wondering at the heavy gold watch chain that curved across her stomach from a pocket on each side of her skirt."

Semester after semester eager learners passed through Ms. Clapp's class. Hannah and her fellow teachers were able to help children absorb the fundamentals of reading, writing, and arithmetic. News of the seminary and the exceptional job being done by Hannah and Elizabeth prompted a visit from Virginia City, Nevada, politician and a member of the House Committee on Colleges and Common Schools, William M. Gillespie. A young Mark Twain was working as a reporter for the newspaper *The Territorial Enterprise* and was sent to cover the event. The article was published on January 14, 1864.

The exercises this afternoon were of a character not likely to be unfamiliar to the free American citizen who has a fair recollection of how he used to pass his Friday afternoons in the days of his youth. The tactics have undergone some changes, but these variations are not important.

In former times a fellow took his place in the luminous spelling class in the full consciousness that if he spelled cat with a "k," or indulged in any other little orthographical eccentricities whereas, he keeps his place in the ranks now, in such cases, and his position, to-day, long after the balance of the class had rounded to, but he subsequently succumbed to the word "nape," which he persisted in ravishing of its final vowel. There was nothing irregular about that. Your rightly constructed schoolboy will spell a multitude of hard words without hesitating once, and then lose his grip and miss fire on the easiest one in the book.

The fashion of reading selections of prose and poetry remains the same; and so does the youthful manner of doing that sort of thing. Some pupils read poetry with graceful ease and correct expression, and others place the rising and falling inflection at measured intervals, as if they had learned the lesson on a "seesaw"; but then they go undulating through a stanza with such an air of unctuous satisfaction, that it is a comfort to be around when they are at it.

> *"The boy-stood-awn-the bur-ning deck–*
> *When-sawl-but him had fled–*
> *The flames-that shook-the battle-zreck–*
> *Shone round–him o'er-the dread."*

That is the old-fashioned impressive style—stately, slow-moving and solemn. It is in vogue yet among scholars of tender age. It always

104

will be. Ever since Mrs. Hemans wrote that verse, it has suited the pleasure of juveniles to emphasize the word "him," and lay atrocious stress upon that other word "o'er," whether she liked it or not; and I am prepared to believe that they will continue this practice unto the end of time, and with the same indifference to Mrs. Heman's opinions about it, or any body's else.

They sing in school, now-a-days, which is an improvement upon the ancient regime; and they don't catch flies and throw spitballs at the teacher, as they used to do in my time—which is another improvement, in a general way. Neither do the boys and girls keep a sharp look-out on each other's shortcomings and report the same at headquarters, as was a custom of by-gone centuries.

Hannah's community influence extended beyond the confines of school. She readily debated the merits of various political candidates, the economy, and women's suffrage with the male leaders of the territory. She was a leading member of a temperance group, supported local charities, both monetarily and with her time, and even had the ear of Senator William Stewart. The accomplished Republican considered Hannah one of his closest advisors. He respected her opinion about the future of education and her opposition to public intoxication. One particular exchange between her and an inebriated man lying outside a saloon demonstrated her strong position against such behavior and how such a scene could affect her students. After witnessing the man stumble out of the tavern and fall into a gutter, she marched to the saloon door and knocked. When the owner of the establishment greeted her, she pointed to his patron and said, "Your sign has fallen down. You'd better prop it up."

The strong-minded, self-reliant teacher organized fundraisers and donated her own land for a larger school to be built in 1865. The Sierra Seminary boarded forty students at that point, and Hannah and her fellow educators were able to teach youngsters facts and skills for decades to come. Hannah and Elizabeth dedicated themselves to the school in Carson City for twenty-five years. By 1887 a quality public school was in place and the seminary was closed. Hannah then relocated to Reno to help establish a university.

Shortly after the first building of the college was erected, Senator William Steward appointed Hannah the first professor. The institution sat on a hill overlooking the fledgling town and had a mere twenty-five students in the first year. Nine of those students were women. Their enrollment made Hannah proud. To her it was a testament of the advancement of women's rights.

The sixty-three-year-old professor of history and English language was devoted to the school. The hours were long and the classrooms were too small, but she found the venture worthwhile. She complained a little when she had to walk to work in the rain and wade through puddles in order to get to her homeroom. She insisted that a great deal of her salary was being spent on overshoes. "When the rains began," she wrote in an article about her life, "we paved the path to class ourselves with overshoes and good intentions."

In the beginning the faculty of the University of Nevada consisted of only the school president, LeRoy Brown, and Hannah. According to Hannah:

This august body presided over the destinies of a microscopic student body, whom it inspired with reverence and awe. But we were not long in want of anything. The people of Reno, in order to have the university, had become responsible for a large sum of money, secured by county bonds.

They were an ambitious and energetic community, who keenly appreciated having a university in their midst, and who inspired

106

the regents to nurse with all care the infant institution. The first addition they made to our faculty was Professor Miller, who came as a special instructor in physiology and as a general all round assistant. Soon followed Professor Jackson from the University of California, who opened the mining department of normal training. There were five of us, representing twice as many departments packed into one building.

Hannah was grateful to the teachers and the pupils and was proud of how well they did with the bare essentials they had to work with at the start, such as no gas and electricity, and limited space. As she later wrote:

It is a joy today to remember the unfailing courtesy, the mutual help-fulness, and good nature that filled the chinks of those close quarters. The students were not one whit behind the teachers, but worked with enthusiasm that was an inspiration. They were thankful for what they got and helped us bear the inconveniences with so kindly a spirit that we actually rejoiced in the circumstances. . . .

Providence has a special care for the young, whether human beings or their creations. Surely it was true of this university. When I think of the fine scholarly work that was done in those early days of this institution and of the enthusiasm, consecration, and special fit-ness of each member of the faculty, it seems it could have been noth-ing sort of a special direction that led to the choice of them. There were not only all the difficulties to be met that attend the beginning of any institution, but also the added difficulties that must attend an institution so isolated a situation. The Sierras shut us in on the Pacific side, and a weary stretch of almost uninhabited plains sepa-rated us from the Atlantic Coast. These were pioneers, indeed, and their spirit was worthy the opportunity.

In addition to her duties as teacher, she served as the vice president of the Nevada Equal Suffrage Association, worked to advance the Republican party, helped found the Nevada Historical Society, and was the preceptress over the girls' cottage at the university. In 1888 she took on the responsibility as school librarian. She took great delight in managing the handful of books and pamphlets the university had acquired. When she left the school fourteen years later, the library's collection had grown to over six thousand books and five thousand pamphlets.

After she had taught more than four years at the university, there were some taxpayers who disapproved of Hannah staying on at the school. They argued that at sixty-seven she was too old to "occupy the position she held." Senator Stewart quickly came to her defense, but the governing board of the school gave in to public opinion and forced her to retire. When Hannah left her post at the University of Reno in 1901, she was honored with a Resolution of Esteem by the Board of Regents. In part the resolution read: "She will retain an honorary position in the University and an active interest in the life and growth of the institution."

Hannah did retain an "active interest" in the life and growth of education, not just that of the university. She created and funded a number of area kindergartens, including one named for her friend and fellow teacher, Elizabeth Babcock. She also served as the President of the Board of Trustees of the Kindergarten Association of Reno. In the later part of 1902, Hannah moved to Palo Alto, California. She made frequent trips to Nevada to oversee the progress and promote the need for kindergartens throughout the state.

Hannah Clapp died at her home on October 8, 1908. Memorial services held at the University of Reno eight days later were attended by several former students, colleagues, and members of the Nevada Historical Society.

The secretary of the organization addressed the mourners and recalled that "Miss Clapp was a pioneer."

"I knew this," he elaborated, "because of the mention made of her in every section of the state. Other women have left their mark on one little community of our Commonwealth, but this one is borne in the hearts of people north, south, east, and west."

The legendary teacher never married and never had any children of her own. She was eighty-four years old when she passed away from natural causes.

Bethenia Owens-Adair

The Student Teacher

"Nothing was permitted to come between me and this, (getting an education) the greatest opportunity of my life."
—*Bethenia Owens-Adair, 1906*

Tears streamed down twelve-year-old Bethenia Owens's face as she watched her teacher pack his belongings into a faded, leather saddlebag and slip his coat on over his shoulder. She was heartbroken that the gracious man who introduced her to the alphabet and arithmetic would be leaving to teach school at a far off location. Bethenia's brothers and sisters gathered around him, hugging his legs and hanging onto his hands. Mr. Beaufort had boarded with the Owens family during the three-month summer school term in 1852, and everyone had grown quite attached to him, especially Bethenia.

Mr. Beaufort smiled sweetly at Bethenia as she wiped her face dry with the back of her dirty hand. Streaks of grim lined her thin features and continued on into her hairline. Her long, brown locks protruded haphazardly out of the pigtails behind each ear. The dainty ribbons that once held her hair in place were untied and dangling down the back of her soiled, well-worn gingham dress.

The teacher stretched out his hand to Thomas Owens, Bethenia's father, and then gave her mother, Sarah, a squeeze around the neck. He thanked them for their hospitality and then turned his attention

Bethenia Owens–Adair

to their nine children. He snatched the youngest child off of the floor, tossed her up and gave the giggling infant a kiss. Mr. Beaufort said goodbye to everyone, but left his farewell to Bethenia for the last.

"I guess I'll take this one with me," he told her mother.

"All right," Sarah replied playfully. "She is such a tomboy I can never make a girl of her anyway."

Bethenia blinked away more tears. Mr. Beaufort took her hand in his and led her out the door. The two walked down the dusty roadway to the gate and continued on for a bit without saying a word. Finally, Mr. Beaufort stopped and bent down next to the faithful student.

"Now little one," he kindly said, "you must go back. You are a nice little girl, and some day you will make a fine woman, but you must remember and study your book hard, and when you get to be a woman everybody will love you, and don't forget your first teacher, will you?"

Mr. Beaufort scooped Bethenia into his arms, kissed her cheek, sat her down in the direction of her home, and went on his way. Bethenia hurried back to the house where she found a quiet spot to cry over the loss of the teacher she so worshipped.

"Of course they all laughed at me," she remembered in her journal years later, "and often times afterward when I was especially rebellious and wayward, which was not infrequently, I would be confronted with, 'I wish the teacher had taken you with him,' to which I never failed to answer promptly and fervently, 'I wish he had too!'"

Bethenia Angelina Owens was born on February 7, 1840, in Van Buren County, Missouri. She was the second oldest child born to a cattle family that emigrated to Clatsop County, Oregon, in 1843. She was an athletic child who roughhoused with her brothers constantly, challenging them to various feats of strength. She did chores around the homestead that were ordinarily reserved for members of the opposite sex and took great pride in the fact that her father referred to her at times as his "boy."

Bethenia was a great help to her mother. Although she was rambunctious and could hold her own against the boys, she was more than capable of looking after her younger siblings while her mother and older sister, Diana, helped work the ranch. According to Bethenia's journal, the job kept her busy. She often had one of her brothers and sisters in her arms and more clinging to her.

"Where there is a baby every two years," she wrote, "there is always no end of nursing to be done; especially when mother's time is occupied, as it was then, every minute, from early morning till late at night, with much outdoor as well as indoor work. She (Bethenia's mother) seldom found time to devote to the baby, except to give it the breast."

By her own account, Bethenia's childhood was mostly idyllic. When the weather was agreeable she spent most of her time outdoors entertaining the little ones she cared for and running and playing with her favorite brother, Flem. She was fond of hunting hens' nests and gathering eggs laid in the most unusual places. She also enjoyed visiting with a neighbor lady who taught her how to cook and sew and told her fairytales during the lessons. Bethenia did not realize her education was lacking until her parents suggested that the Owens children attend school, but she was excited about the prospect.

Children over the age of four were the first to be enrolled at the school in Clatsop County. Older boys and girls, fourteen or fifteen years old, came to class once their chores were completed and took them up again once they were dismissed for the day. Schoolbooks were in short supply and many of the pupils had to share the limited copies of the readers and spellers with one another. The Owens clan took turns studying from the solitary book they borrowed from a family in a neighboring county.

Mr. Beaufort proved to be an exceptional educator for the young in the small Oregon community. Bethenia was smitten with him from their first meeting.

"The new teacher was a find, handsome young man," she wrote in her memoirs, "who held himself aloof from the young people of his age, and kept his person so clean, neat and trim that the country men disliked him."

He interacted with his students, not only during class time, but at recess as well. He played games with the children and gave them the individual attention needed to learn the daily lessons in reading and writing. He had a particular fondness for Bethenia. Not only did he help her with her schoolwork, but he taught her a great deal about horses. She loved to ride, and Mr. Beaufort coached her on the best way to lasso a horse and spring onto its back.

The innocent infatuation Bethenia had for her teacher knew no bounds. Her older sister and mother would periodically admonish her for "always tagging him around." Bethenia wrote that her mother would scold her saying, "You ought to know that he must get tired of you and the children sometimes." Nothing could dissuade her from following after Mr. Beaufort every chance she got, however. She would walk two miles to school with him each morning and late in the afternoon she would haul her siblings to the spot where the teacher would be grading papers.

It took Bethenia a long time to recover after Mr. Beaufort left the Owens homestead. Several years would pass before she would be able to attend school again. But the fire for learning had been ignited and would ultimately be the key to Bethenia's success.

Although she would have much preferred to marry a man like Mr. Beaufort, two years after meeting her beloved teacher Bethenia found herself betrothed to one of her father's ranch hands. She was barely fourteen when she made the acquaintance of Legrand Hill.

He had been living in the Rogue River Valley for a year working his parents' land. He was a handsome man, broad-shouldered and tall. When she looked into her eyes, she saw the promise of a long and happy life. Her parents had selected this man to be her husband, and she trusted their decision. On their recommendation she eagerly placed her future in Legrand's hands.

On May 4, 1854, the petite teenager, dressed in a sky-blue wedding dress, stood next to her groom and promised to be a faithful wife. After the ceremony the pair retired to their home in the middle of 320 acres of farmland Legrand had purchased on credit. The newlyweds lived four miles from Bethenia's parents and in the beginning, all was right with the world. Family and friends visited often, helping Legrand work the property and assisting Bethenia as she made repairs to their small log cabin.

Legrand was an avid hunter, and in between planting and tending to the livestock, he spent days in the forest bagging grouse and deer. Before long, Legrand's hunting trips became an obsession. More often than not, he put off doing chores to track wild game. He idled away so much time, Bethenia's father was forced to complete the job of putting up a good winter house to protect his daughter from the elements. A mere nine months after the wedding, Bethenia had fully recognized in Legrand a "lack of industry and perseverance."

Legrand was opposed to doing an honest day's work and because of that, he was unable to pay the $150 mortgage on the farm. The Hills were forced to sell the land and move to Jackson County, Oregon, to live with Legrand's Aunt Kelly.

Less than a year after the Hills were married, Bethenia gave birth to a boy. The proud couple named the child George. Legrand's slothful ways, however, did not change with the advent of fatherhood. He continued to fritter away his time, leaving the responsibility of earning an income to Bethenia. Her parents paid the young mother a visit and were appalled by the "hand to mouth" living situation in which they found their daughter and grandchild. Thomas managed to persuade his son-in-law to return to Clatsop County. He lured the less than ambitious Legrand back with an offer to give him an acre of land and material to build a house.

Legrand's attitude toward work remained the same in Clatsop County. Against the advice of his father-in-law, he agreed to partner in a brick-making business. He turned what little money he and Bethenia had over to his two partners and then spent all of his time overseeing the venture. He decided against building a home for his wife and child and chose instead to move his family into a tent. A sustained torrential downpour halted the making of the bricks and eventually put an end to the business altogether.

In late November Bethenia contracted typhoid fever. She was much too sick to care for her baby or work to keep food on the Hill table. Her parents stepped in and moved Bethenia and George out of the damp tent and into their dry home.

Thomas pleaded with Legrand to start construction on a house for his family, but he refused to do so until the deed to the land was turned over to him. When Thomas refused to give in to his request, Legrand became furious and decided to build a house in town instead. He proved to be a poor carpenter and after four months the home was still not complete. Wife and child were moved in anyway.

Bethenia continued to struggle with her health. The fever had left her weak and unable to do everything she once did. George was sickly too, but was nonetheless a big eater. Legrand had little or no patience with his three-year-old son's ailments. He spanked him quite frequently for whimpering, and in many instances, was generally abusive toward the toddler.

"Early one morning in March," Bethenia recalled in 1906, "after a tempestuous scene of this sort, Mr. Hill threw the baby on the bed, and rushed downtown. As soon as he was out of sight, I put on my hat and shawl, and gathering a few necessaries together for the baby, I flew over to my father's house."

Sarah Owens applauded her daughter's courage in leaving Legrand.

"Any man that could not make a living with the good starts and help he has had, never will make one," she told Bethenia. "And with his temper, he is liable to kill you at any time."

Bethenia remained at her parents' home even though Legrand made numerous appeals to win her back.

"I told him many times," she later wrote in her journal, "that if we ever did separate, I would never go back and I never will."

After four years of living in a difficult marriage, Bethenia filed for divorce. Many Clatsop County residents were shocked by her actions, and her sister advised Bethenia to "go back and beg him on your knees to receive you."

The forlorn mother refused. "I was never born to be struck by moral man," she insisted.

It was difficult at first, but Bethenia and George's life away from Legrand and his tyrannical behavior proved to be best for mother and son. George thrived under his grandparents' roof, basking in the constant attention he received from his many aunts and uncles. Bethenia used the time and the renewal of her health to attend school in the nearby town of Roseburg. She could barely read or write and believed the only way to improve her condition in life was to get a full education. At the age of eighteen she enrolled in school and shared a third grade class with children who were ten and eleven years younger than her.

She eventually moved out of her parents' home, and, in addition to continuing on with school, focused on a way to support herself and her son.

"I sought work in all honorable directions, even accepting washing," Bethenia noted in her journal, "which was one of the most profitable occupations among the few considered 'proper' for women in those days."

Bethenia's parents objected to her living on her own. They wanted their daughter to stay home and let them care for her and her baby, but she refused. She did accept the sewing machine her parents gave her and, after teaching herself how to use it, added mending to her list of services for hire.

In the fall of 1860, Bethenia traveled to Oysterville, Washington, to visit a friend and decided to stay in the area awhile and attend school. Well-meaning family members urged her to return to Oregon, but she wouldn't agree to do so until after she completed the basic primary grades.

"I now know that I can support and educate myself and my boy, and am resolved to do it," she noted in her journal. "And furthermore, I do not intend to do it over a washtub either."

Bethenia worked her way through primary school by doing laundry for ranch hands. Through books and diligent studying she overcame the hardships associated with a failed marriage and single parenthood. In 1874, she wrote, "Thus passed one of the pleasantest and most profitable winters of my life, while, whetted by what it fed on, my desire for knowledge grew stronger."

An urgent plea from her sister ultimately persuaded her to leave Oysterville and move back to Clatsop County. Bethenia agreed to help her ailing sister in exchange for the chance to attend and teach school in Astoria.

"Don't you think I could teach a little summer school here on the plains?" she asked Diana. "I can rise at four, and help with the milking, and get all the other work done by 8 a.m., and I can do washing mornings and evenings, and on Saturdays."

Diana encouraged her to try and Bethenia quickly hopped on her horse and made the rounds to the various neighbors' homes looking for students.

Bethenia recalled:

I succeeded in getting the promise of sixteen pupils for which I was to receive $2 for three months. This was my first attempt to instruct others. I taught my school in the old Presbyterian church—the first Presbyterian church building ever erected in Oregon. Of my sixteen pupils, there were three who were more advanced than myself, but I took their books home with me nights, and, with the help of my brother-in-law, I managed to prepare the lessons beforehand, and they never suspected my incompetence. From this school I received my first little fortune of $25; and I added to this by picking wild black berries at odd times, which found a ready sale at fifty cents a gallon.

By 1861, Bethenia had earned enough money to purchase her own plot of land in Astoria and build a house.

No amount of hard work could deter Bethenia from achieving her goal of getting an education. She passed from one class to another, moving on to more advanced courses along the way. She admitted that she made it through not because she was the most clever, but because she was determined and refused to give up.

"At 4 a.m. my lamp was always burning," she wrote in her memoirs, "and I was poring over my books—never allowing myself more than eight hours sleep."

Bethenia's thirst for knowledge did not subside after she graduated from high school. The fondness she had as a youngster for nursing and caring for sick friends and family sparked a desire to study medicine. Her superior talent in hat design and dressmaking helped her to raise the necessary funds to attend medical school. She became truly committed to the calling after witnessing an elderly doctor's inability to care properly for a small child.

"The old physician in my presence," she wrote years later, "attempted to use an instrument for the relief of the little sufferer, and, in his long, bungling, and unsuccessful attempt he severely lacerated the tender flesh of the poor little girl. At last, he laid down the instrument, to wipe his glasses.

"I picked it up saying, 'Let me try, Doctor,' and passed it instantly, with perfect ease, bringing immediate relief to the tortured child."

That momentous event set in motion the course of Bethenia's new profession.

Words of encouragement for Bethenia's new aim were few and far between, however. In fact, once she made her career plans known, only two people supported her. One was a trusted physician, who loaned her his medical books; the other was a judge, who applauded her ambition and assured her that she "would win." Most of Bethenia's family and friends were opposed to her becoming a doctor. They sneered and laughed and told her it was a disgrace for a woman to enter into such work. Bethenia disregarded their warnings and criticism and pressed on toward her objective.

Bethenia began her studies at the Philadelphia Eclectic School of Medicine in 1870. Students at the college learned ways to treat the sick using herbs, mineral baths, and natural medicines. Upon graduation she opened a practice in the Portland area. Several patients sought out her unorthodox method of dealing with sickness and pain, and in no time, her business was making a profit. Bethenia could then afford to send nineteen-year-old George to the University of California Berkeley Medical School. He graduated in 1874. Although Doctor Owens's eclectic medical practice was prosperous, she was not satisfied. She pined for more knowledge in her chosen field.

On September 1, 1878, she left Portland for Philadelphia to seek counsel from a professor at her former college. She was advised to attend the University of Michigan, and she left at once to enroll. Her daily schedule was filled with lectures, clinics, laboratory work, and examinations. Bethenia was so engrossed in her studies that she did not hear the bell ring between classes. She never tired of the learning process, and she never suffered with a day of sickness.

In June of 1880, Doctor Owens received her second degree. After graduation she traveled with one of her classmates to do field work in hospitals and clinics in Chicago. In the fall of that same year, she returned to the University of Michigan, accompanied by her son. Together, the mother and son doctors attended advanced lectures in obstetrics and homeopathic remedies. At the conclusion of the lectures, she and George took a trip through Europe. Afterwards, she settled briefly in San Francisco. It was there she met her second husband.

Before she met Colonel John Adair, Bethenia maintained that she was fully committed to her profession and not interested in marriage. A brief courtship with the handsome Civil War veteran changed her mind. The two were married on July 24, 1884, in Portland, Oregon.

Three years after the wedding, the Adairs were expecting their first child. Bethenia boasted in her journal that she was happier than she had ever been before. Her elation would not last long.

"At the age of forty-seven," she wrote, "I gave birth to a little daughter; and now my joy knew no limit, my cup of bliss was full to overflowing. A son I had, and a daughter was what I most desired.... For three days only, was she left with us, and then my treasure was taken from me, to join the immortal hosts beyond all earthly pain and sorrow."

Bethenia found solace from the grief of her daughter's death in caring for the sick in her Portland practice. No matter what the weather conditions were, she never refused a call from a patient since she knew that there was no other doctor within a 200-mile radius.

She attended to all those in need, at times traveling through dense undergrowth and swollen rivers.

Never content with being solely a physician, Bethenia became a student again in 1889 and enrolled in a Chicago medical school, seeking a post-graduate degree. After she completed her studies, she returned home to her husband and the teenage son they had adopted. Her practice continued to grow, and before long she found she could not keep up with her professional work and maintain a home for her family. She chose the practice over her marriage and sent John away to a farm they owned in Astoria. The Adairs' marriage ended in 1903.

At the age of sixty-five, Bethenia retired from her practice. Her focus shifted from day-to-day medical treatment to research. In addition to her research, she worked as a lobbyist for the Women's Christian Temperance Union. She remained a staunch social and political activist until 1926, when she died of natural causes at the age of eighty-six.

The impact Mr. Beaufort had on Bethenia's early years lasted a lifetime. According to her memoirs, he instilled in her a love for learning and was the example of the kind of educator she herself eventually became.

Appendix

Readers and Spellers

One of the first and only textbooks children used in classrooms across the frontier was the McGuffey Reader. Written by Rev. Dr. William Holms McGuffey, a Pennsylvania-born educator and president of Ohio University, the material introduced children to a series of characters that were honest, truthful, and kind. The easy to follow, predominately one-syllable-word fables of people of every age and from every walk of life helped pupils master the alphabet. Teachers had students first spell each word in the tale, pronounce each syllable, and then the word. The following example included in an original edition of the reader from 1836, illustrates the method of presenting words.

> *I like to see a lit–tle dog,*
> *And pat him on the head;*
> *So pret–ti–ly he wags his tail*
> *When–ev–er he is fed.*

The book contained a total of fifty-five stories. The 1844 edition included the tale of a lame dog that, when cured, brought another lame dog to be doctored; of a kind boy who freed his caged bird; of the boy who told a lie and repented after he was found out; and of the chimney sweep who was tempted to steal a gold watch but put it back and was thereafter educated by its owner. Almost every lesson had a clearly stated moral. The stories resonated with students and were remembered by many long after they had left school. According to a graduate from a log cabin school in Texas in 1850, the tales stayed with him for years.

Appendix

As Isaac Babcock recalled in his memoirs:

One story was about two boys,. one reckless and wasteful, and the other careful and economical. The wasteful boy threw away a piece of whip-cord; the careful boy saved his piece, which enabled him later to win in several contests, and his example caused the careless boy to reform. The moral of that story remained with me, and to this day I cannot throw away a good string without recalling the story. There was another story about a little girl who wrote to her aunt and spelled so badly that her letter caused trouble and misunderstanding. And there was a little boy named Hugh who disliked his teacher, Mr. Toil, so he ran away from school. On his journey he met Mr. Toil at every turn. Not until I was older did I understand the story had another meaning.

The McGuffey Readers were published by Truman and Smith Publishers. There were four volumes in the series. The first two books were released in 1836, and the remaining two were released eighteen months later.

In 1834, businessmen and book salesmen, William B. Truman and Winthrop B. Smith, recognized a demand for educational books in a western market. They believed the frontier would expand greatly in the coming decades and that hundreds of families would flood the lands west of Independence, Missouri.

After an extensive search for a teacher who could create quality readers, Truman and Smith decided on Rev. McGuffey. The reverend was very well respected by his students and peers. He was known by all as a spiritual man with an unassuming manner and clear thought, and was highly recommended for the job by his good friend, Harriet Beecher Stowe. McGuffey believed that teachers should study the daily lessons in the book as well as their students and suggested they read aloud to their classes. He also encouraged them to ask the class the questions he had listed in the book after each story. He believed in order for a teacher to give instruction, one must ask questions.

McGuffey Readers have been revised many times to reflect geographical, cultural, and political changes. For more than 170 years the McGuffey Readers have played a part in the education of millions of citizens from New York to California.

One of the most popular stories included in the McGuffey Readers was a tale entitled "I Pity Them." The story centered around the sad fate of an emigrant family who was trying to make its way west when tragedy occurred. According to the authors of the lesson and the preface found in the front of all readers, stories like "I Pity Them"

Courtesy of Library of Congress, LC=65262=86759

This fanciful drawing was used as an illustration for the story "I Pity Them," which appeared in McGuffey Readers in 1879.

were written to "impart valuable information and to exert a decided and healthful moral influence." They maintained that "the preliminary exercises were amply sufficient for drills in articulation, inflection, etc. . . ." The preface further notes that, "a full understanding of the text is necessary in order to read it properly. Full explanatory notes were added at the conclusion of a particular story in hopes that it would add not only to the interest of the reading material, but also to its usefulness from an instructive point of view."

Definitions of the more difficult words in "I Pity Them" were provided at the end of the story, and the pronunciation of the words were indicated by diacritical marks. Illustrations were provided by the most celebrated designers and engravers of the country. "I Pity Them" first appeared in the readers in 1879.

XXI.
"I Pity Them"

1. A poor man once undertook to emigrate from Castine, Me., to Illinois. When he was attempting to cross a river in New York, his horse broke through the rotten timbers of the bridge, and was drowned. He had but this one animal to convey all his property and his family to his new home.

2. His wife and children were almost miraculously saved from sharing the fate of the horse; but the loss of this poor animal was enough. By its aid the family, it may be said, had lived and moved; now they were left helpless in a land of strangers, without the ability to go on or return, without money or a single friend to whom to appeal. The case was a hard one.

3. There were a great many who "passed by on the other side." Some even laughed at the predicament in which the man was placed; but by degrees a group of people began to collect, all of whom pitied him.

4. Some pitied him a great deal, and some did not pity him very much, because, they said, he might have known better than to try to cross an un-safe bridge, and should have made his horse swim the river. Pity, however, seemed rather to predominate. Some pitied the man, and some the horse; all pitied the poor, sick mother and her six children.

5. Among this pitying party was a rough son of the West, who knew what it was to migrate some hundreds of miles over new roads to locate a des-titute family on a prairie. Seeing the man's forlorn situation, and looking around on the by-standers, he said, "All of you seem to pity these poor people very much, but I would beg leave to ask each of you how much."

6. "There, stranger," continued he, holding up a ten dollar bill, "there is the amount of my pity; and if others will do as I do, you may soon get another pony. God bless you." It is needless to state the effect that his active charity produced. In a short time the happy emigrant arrived at his destination, and he is now a thriving farmer, and a neighbor to him who was his "friend in need, and a friend indeed."

Definitions - 1. Em'i-grate, to remove from one country or state to an-other for the purpose of residence, to migrate. *2. Mi-rac'u-lous-ly,* as if by miracle, wonderfully. *A-bil'i-ty,* power, capability. *3. Pre-dic'a-ment,* condition, plight. *4. Pre-dom'i-nate,* to prevail, to rule. *5. Lo'cate,* to place. *Des'ti-tute,* needy, poor. *6. Des-ti-na'tion,* end of a journey. *Thriv'ing,* prosperous through industry, economy and good management.

A Framework for Education in the West

In 1851, California's legislature met to design a framework for instruction for schools in the state. Using the example politicians set for schools in New York and Boston, representatives drafted a "system of common schools." Other western states soon followed suit. The elements of the statutes included provisions for students and teachers alike. The 1864 version of the California statutes also outlined rules for classroom conduct and for maintaining the school register.

Statute 1665—Instruction must be given in the following branches, in the several grades in which each may be required: Reading, writing, orthography, arithmetic, geography, grammar, history of the United States, elements of physiology and hygiene, with special instruction as to the nature of alcoholic drinks and narcotics, and their effects upon the human system, vocal music, elementary bookkeeping, industrial drawing and civil government; provided, that instruction in physiology and hygiene, elementary bookkeeping, and civil government may be oral, no text-books in these subjects being required to be purchased by the pupils.

Statute 1687—In all schools having more than two teachers, beginners shall be taught by teachers who have had at least two years experience.

Statute 1696—Every teacher in the public school must: First—Before assuming charge of a school, file his or her certificate with the Superintendent of Schools.

Second—Before taking charge of a school, and one week before closing a term of school, notify the County Superintendent of such fact, naming the day of the opening or closing. Boards of Education and Boards of School Trustees must in every case give to the teacher a notice of at least two weeks of their intention to close the term of school under their charge.

Third—Enforce the course of study, the use of the legally authorized text-books, and the rules and regulations prescribed for school.

Fourth—Hold pupils to a strict account for their conduct on the way to or from school, on the playgrounds, or during recess; suspend, for good cause, any pupil from the school, and report such suspension to the Board of School Trustees or City Board of Education for review.

Fifth—Keep a state school register, in which shall be left at the close of the term, a report showing a program of recitations, classification, and grading of all pupils who have attended school at any time during the school year."

These statutes formed the basis of a consistent, lasting school-system for the State of California.

Long-term financing for free schools was an uncertain venture, however. Support was dependent on how well the local economy was doing. In order to keep schools continually operating localities would have to rely on the state government. Years before this system could take hold, though, California needed ambitious and caring teachers to help convert the wild mining camps into safe and progressive settlements and towns.

Catherine Beecher: Educational Pioneer

As a teacher herself in Connecticut, Catherine took up the cause of educational reform and the promotion of women as school teachers. The country was growing and men were leaving the field and venturing into areas of business and industry. Catherine recognized the need for women in the vocation and campaigned for the wider education of females to fill the increasing demand. She enrolled numerous women into the school she founded in 1823, the Hartford Female Seminary. Students were taught how to be mothers and teachers. Catherine maintained that the "work of a teacher was more important to society than that of a lawyer or doctor."

Massachusetts born educator Mary Lyon believed women teachers were "vital for the growth of a civilized society." She became an authority on the training of women for the profession. After serving as a vice principal at Ipswich Female Seminary in Massachusetts, she worked tirelessly for three years to create a school to train ladies to be teachers that would rival any that men freely attended. When Mount Holyoke opened its doors in November 1837, the curriculum was equivalent to those at men's colleges. Mary made it affordable for women to attend as well and had the backing of many prominent scholars dedicated to seeing the school thrive. Mount Holyoke provided the inspiration, the model, and often the leadership for many women's colleges to come.

Graduates from Mary Lyon's and Catherine Beecher's schools enthusiastically accepted teaching jobs offered along the East Coast. Catherine was concerned about the growing population settling in land west of Independence, Missouri. After poring over newspaper and magazine accounts about the migration to Oregon and California, Catherine estimated there were thousands of children lacking a place to go for a formal education.

The staggering realization prompted her to form the National Popular Education Board and recruit willing ladies to travel across the plains to teach school. Those who accepted the task were asked to serve a two-year term. Board members helped find positions for the teachers and furnished them with funds to get them to their destinations. Only single women were allowed to participate in the program. The board wanted to keep families intact and felt a husband and children would distract the teachers from their primary objective.

Teaching provided ambitious women with income and stability. Many educators used their wages to purchase homesteads in the areas where they were employed. Some used their pay to buy their own businesses or small homes. Several teachers met and fell in love with settlers who were living and working near them. Once they were married they retired from the field to become homemakers. As a result there was a large turnover in the profession. The National Popular Education Board was faithful to the call to school all children beyond the Mississippi and continually sent educators west to replace the women who had left the jobs.

RULES FOR TEACHERS
1872

1. *Teachers each day will fill lamps, clean chimneys.*

2. *Each teacher will bring a bucket of water and a scuttle of coal for the day's session.*

3. *Make your pens carefully. You may whittle nibs to the individual taste of the pupils.*

4. *Men teachers may take one evening each week for courting purposes, or two evenings a week if they go to church regularly.*

5. *After ten hours in school, the teachers may spend the remaining time reading the Bible or other good books.*

6. *Women teachers who marry or engage in unseemly conduct will be dismissed.*

7. *Every teacher should lay aside from each pay a goodly sum of his earnings for his benefit during his declining years so that he will not become a burden on society.*

8. *Any teacher who smokes, uses liquor in any form, frequents pool or public halls, or gets shaved in a barber shop will give good reason to suspect his worth, intention, integrity and honesty.*

9. *The teacher who performs his labor faithfully and without fault for five years will be given an increase of twenty-five cents per week in his pay, providing the Board of Education approves.*

The National Popular Education Board issued a list of behavioral standards for teachers in 1872.

School Rules

Teachers on the frontier often used any facility available for a classroom: canvas tents, sod houses, barns, or abandoned mining shacks. Supplies were limited. Where readers were absent, Bibles and Sears, Roebuck Catalogs were used to teach children how to read and write. Depending on the size of the town or the mining camp, class size could be as little as three and as many as fifty. Pupils from grades one to eight congregated together in one room. Younger students sat in the front, and older ones were in the back. Girls were on one side, and boys were on the other. The curriculum focused on the basics: reading, spelling, penmanship, arithmetic, and history. Ten- to fifteen-minute sessions were dedicated to each grade level.

The length of the school terms was dictated by the farming families. The children of farmers needed to be available to help their parents with the planting and the harvest. A school year was generally twelve weeks long and ran from Thanksgiving to early spring.

There were stiff penalties for pupils who talked out of turn or forgot to hand in a lesson. Disciplinary measures ranged from standing in the corner and staying after school, to spankings with rulers or hickory switches. Often times the most serious offenders were expelled before corporal punishment was initiated.

At the end of the year it was customary for many frontier schools to invite parents and townspeople to join the students in a celebratory banquet. School patrons and mothers of students brought baskets filled with food. Before anyone could enjoy the meal the pupils would reiterate for the guests all they had learned during the term and share the kind thoughts they had about their long-suffering teachers.

Bibliography

GENERAL REFERENCES

Bettman, Otto L. *The Good Old Days—They Were Terrible!* New York: Random House, 1974.

Brown, Dee. *The Gentle Tamers: Women of the Old Wild West.* Lincoln: University of Nebraska Press, 1958.

———. *Wondrous Times on the Frontier.* New York: Harper Perennial, 1992.

Center for Digital Discourse & Culture History of the McGuffey Readers. http://www2.cddc.vt.edu.

Dary, David. *Seeking Pleasure in the Old West.* New York: Knopf, 1995.

Fuller, Wayne. *One-Room Schools in the Middle West.* Lawrence: University of Kansas Press, 1994.

Herr, Pamela. "*School Days on the Frontier.*" *The American West Magazine,* Buffalo Bill Historical Center, Cody, WY, no. 5, September/October 1978.

Hoffman, Nancy. *Woman's True Profession: Voices from the History of Teaching.* New York: The Feminist Press, 1981.

Homestead History. www.pbs.org/wnet/frontierhouse/frontierlife.

Jupo, Frank. *The Story of the Three R's.* Englewood Cliffs, NJ: Prentice-Hall, Inc., 1970.

Katz, William Loren. *Black Women of the Old West.* New York: Atheneum Books, 1995.

———. *The Black West.* New York: Harlem Moon, Broadway Books, 2005.

Kaufman, Polly Welts. *Women Teachers of the Frontier.* New Haven, CT: Yale University Press, 1984.

Luchetti, Cathy. *Children of the West: Family Life on the Frontier.* New York: W.W. Norton & Company, 2001.

Luchetti, Cathy, and Carol Olwell. *Women of the West.* New York: Crown Trade Paperbacks, 1982.

Swallow, Joan Reiter. *The Women.* Alexandria, VA.: Time-Life Books, 1978.

Waerenskjold, Elise. *The Lady with the Pen.* New York: Arno Press, 1979.

Wallace, Robert. "The Frontier's Fabulous Women." *Life,* May 11, 1959.

Ward, Geoffrey C. *The West: An Illustrated History.* New York: Little, Brown & Company, 1996.

Weeks, Clara A. "Early Schools of Nevada County." *Nevada County Historical Society* 10, no. 2, April 1956.

SISTER BLANDINA SEGALE

Catholic Diocese. www.dcdiocese.org.

Catholic Heritage Curricula. www.chcweb.com.

Segale, Sister Blandina. *At the End of the Sante Fe Trail.* Milwaukee: The Bruce Publishing Company, 1948

MARY GRAVES CLARKE

Bancroft, Hubert Howe. *Annals of the California Gold Era.* Berkeley, CA: The Bancroft Company, 1918.

Foley, D. "Heroine of the Donner Party." *Nevada County Historical Society Bulletin*, August 3, 1964.

McClatchy, C. K. *Early Day Romances Sutter's Fort 1847-1848*. Sacramento, CA: Nugget Press, 1943.

McGlashan, Charles. *History of the Donner Party*. Palo Alto, CA: Stanford University Press, 1940.

Stewart, George R. *Ordeal by Hunger*. New York: Henry Holt & Company, 1936.

ELIZA MOTT

Bancroft, Hubert Howe. The Works of Hubert Howe Bancroft Vol. XXV, History of Nevada, Colorado, Wyoming, 1540-1888. San Francisco: The History Company Publishing, 1890.

Dangberg, Grace and Beatrice Jones. *The Motts of Mottsville*. Carson City, NV: Carson Valley Historical Society article, 1974.

Goddard, George. "The First Records of Carson Valley, Utah Territory." *Nevada Historical Society Quarterly* 9 nos. 2,3, 1966.

Seagraves, Anne. *Women of the Sierra*. Lakeport, CA: WESANNE Enterprises, 1990.

ANNA WEBBER

Kansas State Historical Society. www.kancoll.org.

Scrimsher, Lila G. "The Diary of Anna Webber: Early Day Teacher of Mitchell County." *Kansas Historical Quarterly*, XXXVIII, no. 3, Autumn 1972..

Webber, Anna. Anna Webber's Personal Diary, 1881.

TABITHA BROWN

Lampman, Sibley. *Wheels West: The Story of Tabitha Brown*. New York: Doubleday & Company, Inc. 1965.

Kion, Mary Trotter. www.mkionwritenow.com.

Terry, John. "Mother Symbol." *The Portland Oregonian Newsletter,* March 31, 2002.

OLIVE MANN ISBELL

Bowman, Mary M. "California's First American School and Its Teacher." *Historical Society of Southern California* 10, 1915-1917.

———. "Olive Isbell." Historical Society Southern California Quarterly 10, September/October 1954.

Fisk, Arthur M. "The Trailblazer." Quarterly Bulletin of California Pioneers of Santa Clara County 3, no. 4, Fall 1963.

Youngs, Audrey. "The First American School Teacher." *Paradise California Newsletter,* April 24, 1981.

LUCIA DARLING

Darling, Lucia. Crossing the Prairies in a Covered Wagon: Lucia Darling's Personal Journal—1863. Coll. no. SC245.

Montana Historical Society. www.his.state.mt.us

Park, S. W. The First School in Montana: S.W. Park (Lucia Darling's niece) Personal Remembrances. Coll. no. SC245.

SARAH ROYCE

Royce, Josiah. *Life & Thoughts of Josiah Royce.* Nashville, TN: Vanderbilt University Press, 1999.

Royce, Sarah. *A Frontier Lady: Recollections of the Gold Rush & Early California.* Lincoln: University of Nebraska Press, 1977.

Bibliography

Mary Gray McLench

Bourke, Paul, and Donald P. Debats. *Washington County.* Baltimore: The John Hopkins University Press, 1995.

McKenzie, James. "Teachers." *Oregon Historical Quarterly* 15, 1914.

Steber, Rick. *Women of the West.* Prineville, OR: Bonanza Publishing, 1988.

Washington County Museum. www.washingtoncountymuseum.org.

Sister Russell & the Sisters of Mercy

Dwyer, Father John T. "St. Patrick's Church, Mt. Saint Mary's Orphanages, Convent and Academy of Grass Valley." *California Nevada County Historical Society* 29, no. 4, October 1975.

Lardner, W. B. and M. J. Brock. History of Placer and Nevada Counties, California with Biographical Sketches. Los Angeles: Historic Record Company, 1924.

Leuteneker, Sibyl L. "California's Pioneer Sister." *Nevada County Historical Society Bulletin* 22, no. 1, March 1968.

Paulette, Sister Mary. "Mount St. Mary's Academy." *Mount Saint Mary's Academy Booklet,* May 28, 1966

Hannah Clapp

Bennett, Dana. "Women in Nevada Politics." *Nevada State Library & Archives Newsletter,* August 1996.

Clapp, Hannah K. "The Spirit of the Pioneers." *Tri-Decennial Celebration Newsletter,* October 13, 1888.

Rocha, Guy and Dennis Myers. "Hannah Clapp & the Capitol Fence." *Sierra Sage Newsletter,* July 2003.

Steele-Carlin, Sherril. "Hannah K. Clapp: Nevada's Pioneer Educator." *Silver & Blue Newsletter,* May/June 1994.

Totton, Kathryn Dunn. "Hannah Keziah Clapp: The Life and Career of a Pioneer Nevada Educator, 1824-1908." *Nevada Historical Society Quarterly* XX, no. 3 (Fall 1977), pp. 166–183.

BETHENIA OWENS-ADAIR

Chaney, Charles C. "Bethenia Owens-Adair: Pioneer Woman Doctor of the Northwest." *The Dameron-Damron Family Newsletter* 33, Fall 2001.

Enss, Chris. *Hearts West: True Stories of Mail-Order Brides on the Frontier.* Guilford, CT: Globe Pequot Press, 2005.

———. *The Doctor Wore Petticoats: Women Physicians of the Old West.* Guilford, CT: Globe Pequot Press, 2006.

Oregon Historical Society. www.ohs.org.

Owens-Adair, Bethenia. *Dr. Owens-Adair: Some of Her Life Experiences.* Portland, OR: Mann & Beach Printers, 1923.

Index

About the Author

Chris Enss is an award-winning screenwriter who has written for television, short-subject films, live performances, and movies. Enss has done everything from stand-up comedy to working as a stunt person at the Old Tucson Movie Studio. She learned the basics of writing for film and television at the University of Arizona, and she is currently working with *Return of the Jedi* producer Howard Kazanjian on the movie version of *The Cowboy and the Senorita*, their biography of western stars Roy Rogers and Dale Evans. Her recent books include *The Doctor Wore Petticoats*, *The Lady Was a Gambler*, and *A Beautiful Mine*.